AF411756

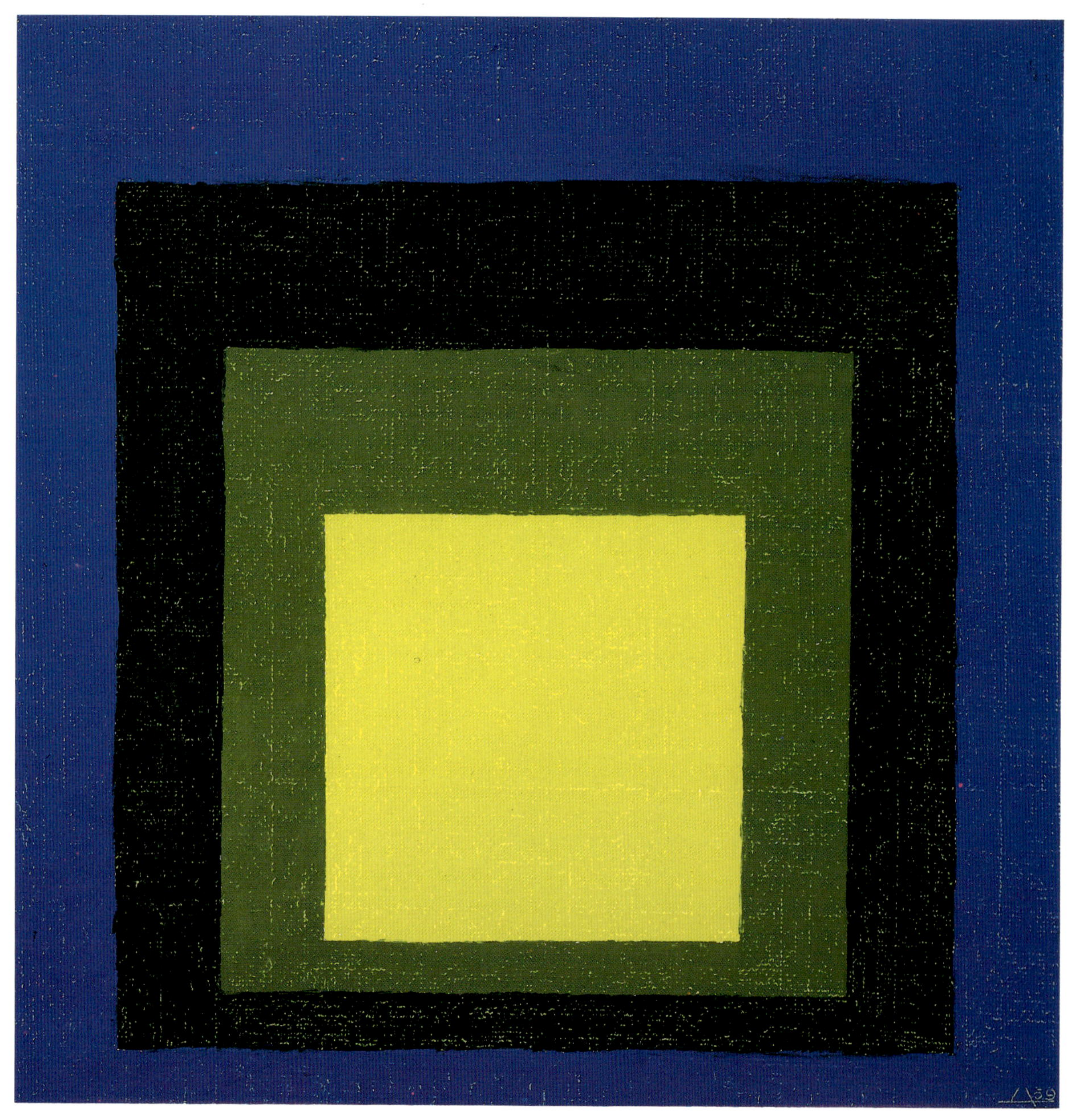

2. Josef Albers, Study for Homage to the Square Blue Spring, 1959

Cincinnati Art Museum

The Alice and Harris Weston

Collection of Post-War Art

November 3, 1989 - January 7, 1990

Contents

Typography and design by Noel Martin
Typesetting by Cobb Typesetting, Inc.
Printed by Sidney Printing Works

Cataloging Notes

Cincinnati Art Museum
    The Alice and Harris Weston collection of post-war art
    p. cm.

    Catalog of an exhibition held at the Cincinnati Art
Museum, November 3, 1989, to January 7, 1990.
    Bibliography:
1. Art, Modern – 20th century – Exhibitions 2. Art,
Modern – Private collections 3. Weston, Alice – Art
collections – Exhibitions 4. Weston, Harris – Art
collections – Exhibitions I. Taylor, Sue II. Title

N 6488.5 W4C5 1989
ISBN 0-931537-11-8

Cover illustration: Hans Hofmann,
Untitled, 1942 (detail)

Foreword

A few years ago, the Cincinnati Art Museum approached Alice and Harris Weston with a proposal to exhibit a large selection of works of art from their collection. The Westons responded generously. Exhibiting a private art collection in a public setting can never illustrate completely the owners' pursuit to acquire, their contacts with dealers and artists, or echo the installation in their home. However, the presentation in museum galleries offers a rare opportunity to change perspective and to share with a wider audience. The Cincinnati Art Museum is deeply indebted to Alice and Harris Weston for lending this exhibition of modern American and European works of art.

Sue Taylor, author of the catalogue's essay, has lectured and written extensively on contemporary art, including articles and reviews for *Art in America, Artnews,* and Chicago's *New Art Examiner.* Presently she serves as visiting associate curator of the David and Alfred Smart Gallery of the University of Chicago. We are grateful for her thoughtful insights and scholarly appraisal of the movements and styles illustrated by works in the Westons' collection.

For the Museum, Genetta Gardner, associate curator of paintings, coordinated the exhibition and its catalogue, and we thank her for shepherding the many steps in planning and presentation. The talented assistance of Museum staff members Dennis Kiel, associate curator of prints, drawings, and photographs; Noel Martin, Museum designer; Carol Schoellkopf, editor and manager of publications production; Ron Forth, photographer; and Mark Rohling, installation designer, has been an invaluable contribution.

Cincinnati has a proud history of art collecting and collectors. The Cincinnati Art Museum is pleased to present this exhibition that joins a prestigious roster stretching back into the mid-nineteenth century. The collecting tradition in Cincinnati thrives and continues.

— Millard F. Rogers, Jr., Director

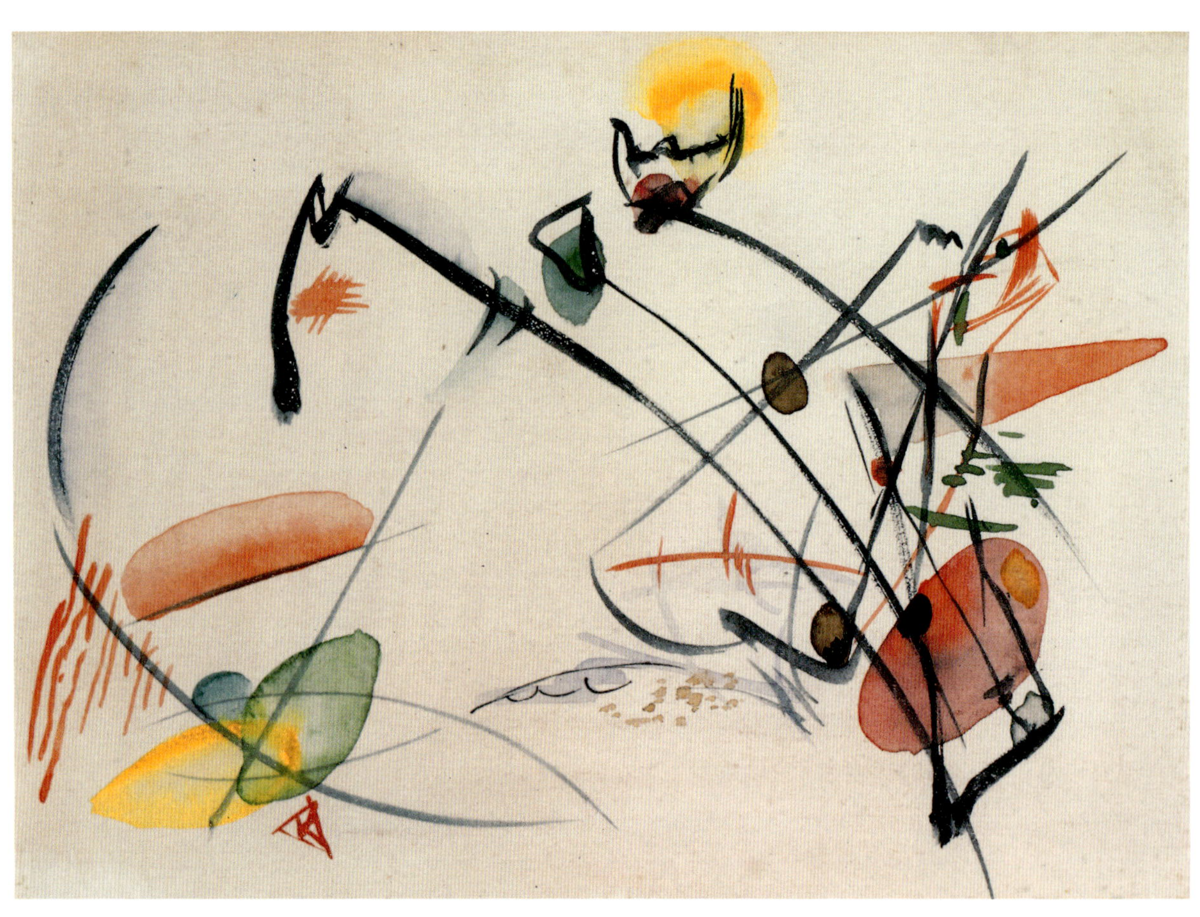

47. Wassily Kandinsky, Simple, 1916

Introduction

It is a pleasure and a privilege for my husband and me to have our art collection exhibited at the Cincinnati Art Museum. We enjoy having people view our collection in our home, and we are especially pleased to be able to share it with a larger audience.

People often ask how we started collecting. One night in the late fifties we saw a group of ten huge Jackson Pollock paintings at the Cincinnati Contemporary Arts Center, when it was still located in the basement of the Cincinnati Art Museum. Their heroic power moved me deeply, and I felt I was in a whole new world. All ten works were owned by one individual, Ben Heller. I realized then that I, too, could own good art. I was excited at the prospect of acquiring art and being able to live with it every day. All I had to do was buy it. For me, it was already too late to buy much Abstract Expressionism. It had become too expensive. At that instant I programmed myself to be psychologically ready for the very next movement that might come along. I resolved to go to New York and buy twenty large canvases at five hundred dollars each, of the very next movement, no matter what it was.

While our collecting did not begin exactly this way, our first Pop art purchase occurred when we were negotiating for a painting of an earlier style. The dealer did not have the work we wanted, but fortuitously, he sent us instead *Box of Shirts* by Claes Oldenburg. We were totally unmoved by it. Nothing had prepared us for its stark objectivity. There was no feeling in it, as in Abstract Expressionism, no personal statement. It was just a common object out there. Well, maybe just a whiff of Dada. It happened to cost five hundred dollars. I took a deep breath and bought it.

Box of Shirts was Pop art, and Pop art turned out to be the next movement. Soon after that the Contemporary Arts Center was getting together a Pop art show, and they gave me letters of introduction to visit the emerging artists of this movement, who were being considered for the show. On my trip to New York I met Jim Dine, Tom Wesselmann, James Rosenquist, and Robert Indiana in their studios. We acquired much of our Pop art then: Wesselmann's *Great American Still Life #6,* Indiana's *Fork,* Dine's *Color Chart* and *Shower* (no. 24). Later, we bought a quintessential Pop piece, Andy Warhol's *Soup Can* and his *Elizabeth Taylor* and *Flowers.*

I was also interested in contemporary music and, because of that, in the mid-1960s, my husband raised money to bring John Cage to Cincinnati. The College Conservatory of Music at the University of Cincinnati wanted him as composer-in-residence. It was my great privilege to host him for six months, introducing him to people and helping him schedule his musical events in the city. John Cage, with his chance procedures derived from oriental philosophy, has been the inspiration of a generation of artists. However, during the six-month period, intense exposure to his very different set of values created a lot of inner turmoil in me. For a Western-oriented, middle-aged Jewish woman with middle-class values, who tries to plan, organize and get everything under control, the emphasis on chance to guide one's musical, and even one's everyday decisions, was diametrically opposed to everything I had been brought up to believe. Those six months were a broadening experience, believe me. Despite his revolutionary ideas, by the end of the semester both my husband and I became very fond of John.

Carl Solway, a fine Cincinnati art dealer, was commissioning artists to do work for his gallery. While John Cage was in Cincinnati, I realized he was basically a philosopher, and could express himself in any medium, not only music. I asked him if he would be interested in doing some lithographs. After hearing his affirmative response, I teamed up with Carl Solway, and we published a portfolio of them.

John used his familiar chance procedures to create a visual instead of an auditory piece. In his explanatory booklet describing the process, he asks a series of questions, has a series of answers available, and then rolls the dice to see which answers determine that particular artistic decision. For example, the editions turned out to be eight plexigrams and two lithographs. Half the edition of 125 were bought by museums. The work is entitled *Not Wanting to Say Anything About Marcel . . . ,* and is dedicated to Marcel Duchamp, whose interest in chance John Cage greatly admired.

John Cage also introduced me to his confreres, Jasper Johns and Robert Rauchenberg. I will never forget Jasper Johns when he greeted John Cage and me at his home. Entering from a small door to the huge living room, which previously had been a bank lobby, he was dressed in a Japanese kimono with a white kitten around his broad shoulders. To his right, covered with a cloth so no one could see, was his as yet unfinished *Voice* painting. Through John Cage, I also met Teeny Duchamp, Marcel's widow, who traded me *Valise* for one of the plexigrams.

I continued to keep an open mind to new movements, in order to buy them early enough while still reasonably priced. The Contemporary Arts Center was a big help in introducing and educating us to new art. Jack Boulton, consultant to the Chase Manhattan Bank Art Collection until his recent untimely death, was the Center's director when I was its president of the Board. He was particularly insistent that we acquire works by Carl Andre and Dorothea Rockburne, rigorous proponents of minimalist art. We listened to his advice. We also added works by George Rickey.

Joseph Albers is a precursor to Minimalism. I met Albers at the *Responsive* Eye show at the Museum of Modern Art years ago. He seemed very pleased to learn that we had purchased his just-published book *Interaction of Color,* although he remained unimpressed that we owned five of his paintings. Enthusiastically, he took me by the hand and guided me to the room in which there were only his *Homage to the Square* paintings. He told me about them, explaining in response to my question that the colors for the paintings were chosen intuitively by him and were not dictated by the scientific knowledge expounded in his book. He also confided that his paintings were different from Agam's, which were hanging nearby. "Agam's change as you physically move past them, but with mine, the movement takes place in your brain," he said. "My *Despite Straight Lines* appear to move because of how the brain perceives images." I was very excited by this unexpected lesson from such a master.

Also a part of the minimalist tradition is Dan Flavin's neon piece, which we have installed against the corner of our garage. It is eight feet high and consists of three tubes, with a blue tube facing the viewer, and green and yellow tubes behind. The light is electrically connected to our garage door, so when we drive in, the Flavin goes on to welcome us. Flavin knows about this installation and has approved our using it in this fashion.

The environmental artists represented in our collection include Robert Smithson, Christo, Alan Sonfist, and me. Smithson is best known for his *Spiral Jetty,* a huge work now under water near Salt Lake City, Utah. We have a little sketch of it. We also have a circle carved into a slab of fossilized rock, a model for a large uncompleted environmental piece similar to Stonehenge.

The most recent movement of which this collection is comprised is Postminimalism. Its characteristics, unlike Minimalism, are unpretentious, modest, and unheroic. It uses materials of bits of wood, wire, or string. We have two related wire pieces in our home which one could easily miss. They are by Richard Tuttle. There is a delicate interplay of interval between the protruding wire, its shadow and a hand-drawn pencil line on the wall. The intervals change as the light changes.

Installation is integral to Tuttle's pieces. When they are moved he likes to reinstall them to ensure their correct installation. Last year, he came to Cincinnati to reinstall the ten small wood segments, the *Cincinnati Pieces,* in the garage. On that trip, Tuttle made up an instruction book, with drawings and photographs, to show exactly how to place the segments in the center of the wall, and at the correct angles, so he does not have to come personally to reinstall them each time they are moved.

These art movements and subsequent ones, with many minor offshoots, have come thick and fast since the fifties. Oftentimes, viewers who do not keep themselves up-to-date on current trends judge later movements with the same criteria as earlier ones. This often leads to frustration and anger. A pure white canvas, for example, can mean many things, depending on its historical perspective. It could mean the promise of a new utopian society if it were done by the Constructivist Malevich in the twenties. It could mean a *tabula rasa* from which aggressive stimuli are withdrawn in order for more subtle environmental stimuli to appear, as in the Eastern-oriented *4 Minutes and 33 Seconds of Silence* by John Cage in the fifties. Or it could mean the stripping away of non-essential details to get down to a powerful basic essence, as in minimal art in the sixties. But, in any case, if one believes any five-year-old could do it, then such a reaction only reflects the lack of understanding by the viewer, who, if informed, might react more positively. Therefore, I highly recommend that when viewing contemporary art, it is absolutely necessary to ascertain the intention of the artist before forming an opinion.

I also have created art of my own. My work has to do with revealing unseen forces of nature. As the scale changes from microcosmic to cosmic, different landscapes are revealed, from the frenzied collision of sub-atomic particles within the atom, through the infinity of shapes, patterns and colors of crystals at a molecular level, to the majesty of the cyclical revolutions of the sun and moon as tracked by prehistoric peoples of the Central Ohio Valley. I have used whatever artistic medium was best suited to reveal these forces, including silkscreen monoprints, sculpture, photography, and multi-media ballet, symphony and videotape.

Even though there are many works of art

represented our collection, there was no
magic involved in acquiring it. Large sums of
money are not required if the art is purchased
early enough. We have made some mistakes,
but that is to be expected. Even starting now,
it is not too late for anyone to collect, if one
concentrates on works by young emerging
artists, who are beginning to receive national
attention.

Contemporary artists have a special
sensitivity to our times which they express
through their art. Therefore, if we have a
contemporary art collection, we have clues to
understanding the epoch in which we live. It
has been a broadening experience and a
tremendous privilege for us to be exposed
daily to these perceptive expressions of our
era. We appreciate being able to share them
with you, and hope that, through this
Cincinnati Art Museum exhibition, you, too,
will find them meaningful.
— Alice Weston

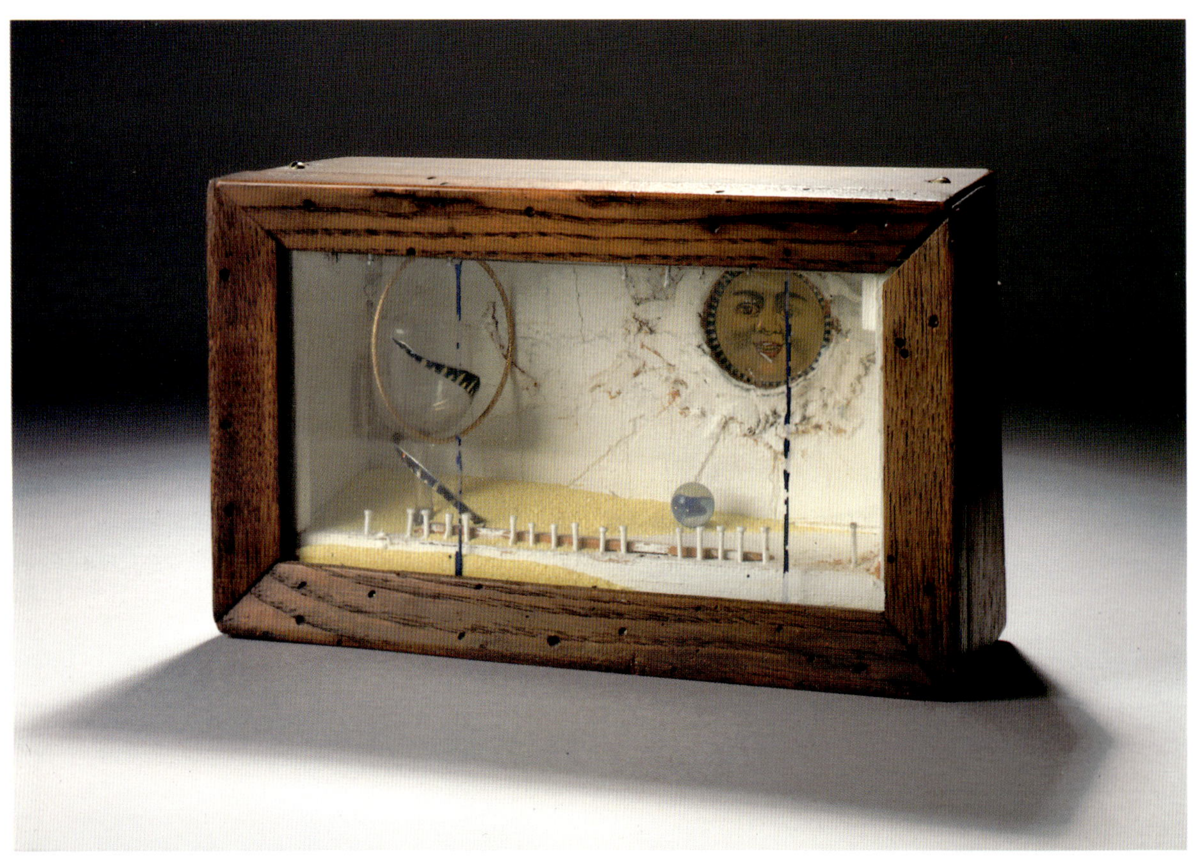

19. Joseph Cornell, The Sun Series, 1957

The Alice and Harris Weston Collection

Serious collectors always maintain a passionate admiration for objects of beauty or historical significance; they may acquire art "to escape the reality around us, to court immortality, to educate, or for sheer pleasure."[1] Collectors of contemporary art are an especially prescient and adventuresome group, for they embrace the new, the unproven, art that is often intellectually and aesthetically challenging in its departures from convention. Alice and Harris Weston are such collectors, having assembled an extraordinary survey of paintings, drawings, prints, and sculpture reflecting the major artistic movements of our time. Perhaps because Alice Weston is herself an artist, interested in the myriad possibilities of diverse types of aesthetic investigation, the Weston collection is not limited to one medium or stylistic point of view. Moreover, her childhood, during which she and her family lived alternately in the Philippines and the United States, prepared her well for adapting to change and taught her an early appreciation for different cultures. Thus in addition to the modern American and European art in this exhibition, the Westons have acquired Philippine tribal sculpture, Eskimo carving, and ancient Near Eastern, Pre-Columbian, and Native American pottery. Harris Weston, whose preferences tend toward ordered and geometrically informed styles, appreciates the benefit to the collection of his wife's eclectic taste.

With few exceptions, the objects the Westons have selected are of an intimate scale; this is truly a collection to be lived with and enjoyed, integrated into daily life in a domestic setting. Although several paintings and prints on view — by Louise Behr, for example, Henry Moore, Georges Rouault, and George Segal — depict human subjects, figuration in general is not a primary focus; instead, abstract, conceptual, and environmental art hold pride of place, and there is a distinct sympathy for primitivism in all its manifestations in modern art. Examples of Abstract

Expressionism, Pop, Minimalism, Postminimalism, and Conceptual art constitute the core of the collection; but other movements – Dada, Surrealism, geometric abstraction, Op and kinetic art – are also represented.

The earliest piece in this exhibition, a beautiful watercolor by Wassily Kandinsky titled *Simple* (1916, no. 47), is the single example of German Expressionism, but its significance within the collection lies more in what it forecasts than what it typifies. Among the first practitioners of abstraction in the twentieth century, Kandinsky believed in the supreme importance of content in a work of art; even when subject matter is apparently lacking in his paintings and drawings of the teens, the artist has invariably inserted veiled references to the apocalypse he hoped was about to usher in a new spiritual age.[2] Works like *Simple*, which at first glance seem to result from some spontaneous expression of the artist's emotional state, are actually fantastic landscapes, with horizons, hills, crumbling towers, rainbows, and celestial orbs, that signal the end of the world as we know it and the dawn of a different era.[3]

Kandinsky contended that art was on a path towards the abstract or non-material; because of this, all the various arts – painting, dance, literature – appeared to him to be drawing closer together, with music, the most abstract, as their model.[4] As an artist Kandinsky did not restrict himself to one medium; his play or "stage composition," *The Yellow Sound*, demonstrates his commitment to the concept of synaesthesia. One is reminded of the later activities of John Cage, a philosopher, musician, and composer who easily translates his ideas into visual art, producing, for instance, the lithographs and plexigrams titled *Not Wanting to Say Anything about Marcel* (1969, no. 13) in the Weston collection. Parenthetically, it was Alice Weston who suggested the lithographic medium to Cage while he was in residence at the University of Cincinnati in the 1960s.

She herself has also overstepped traditional artistic boundaries; educated in graphic design, she has employed photography, video, and computer technology in works such as *Liquid Crystal Light Box* (1971-74) and in the dramatic *Inner Journey* (1987), in which music and abstract visual imagery combine to provide an evocative aesthetic experience.

An early precedent for multi-media experiments, *The Yellow Sound* was first published in *The Blue Rider Almanac*, edited by Kandinsky and his friend Franz Marc, in 1912.[5] The almanac is also important for its juxtapositions, in reproductions, of Malayan sculpture, African masks, Bavarian and Russian folk art, and children's drawings, as well as paintings by the contemporary avant garde. Kandinsky's transcultural approach, his positioning of ethnographic materials on the same plane with "official" European art, finds an echo in the Westons' embrace of tribal artifacts along with the "high art" of Western culture. It is not surprising to find in the collection several pieces by the Puerto Rican-born Rafael Ferrer, an essentially self-taught artist and professional musician, whose anthropological themes and combinations of primitive and high-tech materials comment on the meeting of tribal and industrial cultures. The colorful *Face* (1973), for example, looks like a ritual mask that might be worn by a shaman but is drawn on a commercial brown paper bag; Ferrer's twelve-foot wooden *Boat* (1972), which could be an aboriginal vessel from some far corner of the globe, is illuminated from within by a lightning bolt of bright red neon.

Ferrer has noted the influence of the Spanish exile E. F. Granell, a surrealist writer and painter whom he met at the University of Puerto Rico in 1953, and of subsequent introductions to André Breton, Wilfredo Lam, and Benjamin Peret in Paris.[6] The Surrealists' affection for primitive art is of course well known, and it is surely within the context of surrealist thought that Jean Dubuffet, often treated as an artist *sui generis*, formulated the ideas on *art brut* articulated in his famous "Anti-Cultural Positions" lecture in 1951.[7] His delightful ink-and-wash drawing in the Weston collection, *Exodus* (1961, no. 25), has an awkward, unrefined quality associated with the positive "savage values" Dubuffet attributed to tribal cultures, children, and the insane. Less obvious is the primitivist attitude that informs his enigmatic "texturologies," represented in this exhibition by three lithographs from 1959, *Jardin de Terre*, *Mycelium*, and *Poudroiement* (no. 29). Part of Dubuffet's admiration for *art brut* stemmed from its apparent recognition of the wondrous in the commonplace aspects of experience. The texturologies, which look like pure exercises in formal abstraction, are actually fond meditations on the humblest subject imaginable – the surface of the earth. Elevating what is literally looked down upon or trodden underfoot, Dubuffet depicts the ground in these prints; their titles, so romantic in French, mean respectively "garden of earth," "fibers of fungus," and "dustiness of the road."

There is a fascinating ambivalence of scale in these texture studies of soils and pavements; it is never clear whether what is presented is an infinitesimal fragment of a field or a glimpse of infinity. "I got the idea," Dubuffet wrote about these unusual landscapes, "that the forms to which living matter is attached are always the same ones, whether we are talking about extremely tiny objects or about great geological developments."[8] Alice Weston has pursued a similar train of thought, independent of Dubuffet, with her microphotographs of crystals, subatomic particles, and body tissues, which she has magnified and incorporated in mixed-media sculptures such as *Inside Tracks* (1988) and *Cellular Landscape* (1971). She has spoken of the existence of "a microscopic world . . . which forms another landscape in its own right," and echoes Dubuffet's observations in a discussion of her "cellular landscape" series:

"From tiny images, taken under a microscope, as these were, to enormous images, taken from outer space, there are similar shapes, patterns, and designs. The smallest bit of human body tissue or fluid, of which these [Plexiglas] sculptures are enlargements, takes on expanses of mountains and rivers, when scale is ambiguous."[9]

Dubuffet's reliance, to a certain degree, on chance procedures to produce his printed textures, his method of collaborating with rather than entirely dominating his materials, is akin to Alan Sonfist's approach in "paintings" like *Heat Interference Pattern* and *Micro-Organisms* (n.d.). In these works, the abstract patterns that appear on the metal plates or canvas result from chemical or biological processes respectively, which the artist has set in motion but whose results he does not ultimately control. Like other postminimal, process art of the 1970s, Sonfist's work can often be read as a document of its own making. *Walking Stone* (1978), for example, consists of the impression left by a pebble the artist rolled across a narrow bed of clay; the completed sculpture includes the pebble itself as well as its ceramic track. With these clues, the viewer is invited mentally to reconstruct the operation by which the piece was fabricated.

In addition to stones, Sonfist has used soil, water, trees, wind, and sun to make art; his work reflects an educated sensitivity to the environment and to natural phenomena (see no. 81). He is one of a number of artists who emerged in the 1970s to abandon the confines of the studio and work in the landscape itself. Many of these artists produced remote earthworks which were then transported back to the gallery or museum in the form of photographs, maps, graphics, and film. Famous for enormous projects like *Valley Curtain* (1971) in Rifle Gap, Colorado, and *Running Fence* (1972-76), which swept across Marin and Sonoma Counties in California, Christo has supported his monumental efforts through the sale of such site documentation in drawings and collage. His *Wrapped Documents* (1983, no. 17) in the Weston collection, a discrete object with precedents in surrealist assemblages such as Joseph Cornell's *Sun Series* (1957, no. 19) or Man Ray's *N for Nothing* (1958), can also be seen as a kind of site-specific piece: it contains the lease agreement of the Contemporary Arts Center in Cincinnati, of which the Westons have long been major supporters.

More directly related to the environmental art of the seventies, however, is the drawing by Robert Smithson for his immense *Spiral Jetty* (1970) in the Great Salt Lake in Utah (no. 77). Although the jetty itself, a fifteen-foot wide path of mud, basalt, and limestone coiling fifteen hundred feet into the lake, has been submerged since 1972, it survives in photos, in a documentary film produced by the artist, and in diagrams such as this one in the Weston collection, an aerial view of the jetty with descriptive notations. The symbolic spiral form pertains on one level to local legends about the Great Salt Lake being connected by a whirlpool to the Pacific Ocean; it also refers to Smithson's theory of entropy, borrowed from thermodynamics, of the "winding down" of all energy systems, which eventually reach a point of equilibrium, stasis, or death. Smithson was fascinated by physics, biology, information theory, geography, and natural history, and he saw the *Spiral Jetty* as an allegory spanning geological time: in this modern ruin, "the far distant past (the beginning of life in saline solutions symbolized by the lake) is absorbed in the remote past (symbolized by the destructive forces of the legendary whirlpools in the lake) and the no longer valid optimism of the near present."[10] Similarly, Smithson's *Circle* (1973) in this exhibition, which consists of a ring inscribed by the artist on a fragment of fossilized shale, conflates the past and the present in a single elemental image, while suggesting something of an atavistic reverence for nature and nature's cycles that has been largely lost in an urban industrial society.

Earthworks like the *Spiral Jetty* exemplify a different kind of primitivism from that offered by Dubuffet, for instance, or Ferrer. Harking back to prehistoric monuments such as Stonehenge or the cryptic lines and pictorial systems inscribed in the earth on the Nazca Plains in Peru, Smithson's jetty postulates an affinity between the neolithic and the now. Other contemporary artists have also been fascinated by such mysterious ancient sites, intrigued by the belief systems that must have informed them, whether religious, scientific, or both. In 1983, when critic Lucy Lippard published *Overlay*, a survey of modern earthworks and performances inspired by the art of prehistory, Alice Weston's aerial photographs of the Nazca lines were used to illustrate the chapter "Time and Again: Maps and Places and Journeys."[11] More recently, and closer to home, Alice Weston has begun to investigate an archaic earthwork at Fort Ancient in Warren County, Ohio, where stone markers from about 1200 A.D. still indicate the respective points on the horizon at which the sun rises on the longest and shortest days of the year. Her color photographs *The First Gleam of Summer* (1985) and *Winter Solstice* (1985, no. 103) document the precise alignments of these primitive calendrical markers, which may have had a sacred or ritualistic significance.

An overlay of the primal and the modern also exists in Willem de Kooning's oil-on-paper *Torso or Cross-Legged Woman* (1965, no. 21), with its ultimate source, like the artist's notorious *Woman* paintings of the early fifties, in paleolithic fertility figurines such as the *Venus of Willendorf*. De Kooning's conception of *Ur*-woman, distilled here to a torso rendered in visceral strokes and splashes of red, yellow, and white, is superimposed on newsprint, a sheet ironically borrowed from the "women's pages" of the *New York Times*. Two printed pictures of demure debutantes still visible at the upper corner of the page serve as vapid foils to the naked sensuality of De Kooning's painted female form. The apparent spontaneity or speed with which he applied the paint implies an emotionality that contrasts sharply with the mechanical process of typesetting and printing the news. Moreover, this speed establishes a tension within the image itself, as always when De Kooning's "underlying interest in velocity [is brought] to bear on the fixity of his iconlike woman images." The result, as artist Budd Hopkins has observed, "is a profoundly unsettling contrast between the stable, ancient, received representation of the earth goddess-mother-female, and a jittery, modern, ambiguous sexual battleground."[12]

The equation of expressive gesture with the content of a work of art was of course the foundation of abstract expressionist painting and sculpture, further represented in the Weston collection by small but powerful untitled works by Franz Kline (1957-58, no. 48) and John Chamberlain (1968) respectively. For the German-born Hans Hofmann, on the other hand, who brought first-hand knowledge of fauve, expressionist, and cubist principles to American artists when he settled permanently in the United States in 1932, painterly gesture was a means for energizing pictorial space. Hofmann's interests were, above all, formal. His dynamic untitled oil of 1942 (no. 42), with its brilliant primary colors, lines and planes all in tense equipoise, demonstrates the artist's well-known "push-pull" theory of composition, and his conviction that any "represented form that does not owe its existence to a perception of movement is not a form, because it is...spiritless and inert."[13]

This interest in the perception of motion in abstract forms was shared by Josef Albers, like Hofmann a European *emigré* who became an influential teacher in the United States. Albers, however, in his celebrated *Homage to the Square* series, eschews painterly facture altogether in favor of pristine, anti-expressive surfaces and hard-edge forms. In paintings like *Study for Homage to the Square Blue Spring* (1959, no. 2) and *Aware* (1960), his concern is directed to the way various hues, when juxtaposed, seem to advance or recede in relation to one another. Through his familiarity with gestalt psychology and the optical effects of color, Albers was able to create the illusion of three dimensions on a two-dimensional plane, with the most economic of means. Strangely, in all his supremely static paintings and prints, "pulsating motion coexists with stillness and calm, animation with serenity."[14] Albers's preoccupation with optical illusion finds a later echo in this exhibition in the striking Op-art prints by Julian Stanczak (1971) and Victor Vasarely (n.d.).

Focused on perceptual issues and color theory rather than the spiritual or sublime, Albers's paintings are impersonal, anonymously crafted, and very different from the deeply subjective works of De Kooning and other artists of the New York School. With his disciplined approach to artmaking and his skills as an educator, Albers attracted a number of students during his tenure at Black Mountain College in North Carolina, including, in 1949, the young Robert Rauschenberg (see no. 63), who had "realized that energy and feelings alone could not get [the artist] past that dead end of material indulgence."[15]. Although he would later rebel against his mentor, Rauschenberg developed crucial and enduring friendships at Black Mountain, especially with Cage and choreographer Merce Cunningham, with whom he would later collaborate as a performer and set and costume designer. Rauschenberg's embossed *Cunningham Relief* (1974) in the Weston collection, depicting two dancers in silhouette, celebrates his long association with the great modern dancer/director portrayed in Andy Warhol's silkscreen print on floral paper, *Merce* (1974).

Cunningham's project was to free dance "from all its non-dance encumbrances – no plot, no storytelling, no...psychological or ritualistic overtones."[16] Similarly, Cage rejected the expression of feelings in music and art; he sought an art from which individual tastes and emotions would be eliminated. Thus, whether composing a score or making a drawing or lithograph, Cage substitutes chance operations for aesthetic decision-making. By consulting star charts, throwing I Ching coins, and relying on computer programs, he has consistently circumvented the element of personal choice in artistic production: "I gave up making choices," he recalls. "In their place I put the asking of questions."[17] The letters and word fragments printed on Plexiglas panels in Cage's *Not Wanting to Say Anything about Marcel* (1969, no. 13) were selected according to numerical charts from predetermined texts — by a roll of the dice. The "Marcel" in the title is of course Marcel Duchamp, whose cut-out profile haunts Jasper Johns's stenciled portrait, *M. D.* (1974), also in this exhibition.

Duchamp's own use of chance to undermine traditional notions of artmaking has influenced several generations of conceptual artists. Significantly, Duchamp figures in the Weston collection with no fewer than five works (see no. 33), one of which, the punning *Czech Check* (1965), attests to his delight in word play and predicts the later verbal/visual palindromes of Bruce Nauman, such as *Caned Dance* (1974). The *Boîte-en-Valise* or *Green Box* (1934) contains a Duchamp retrospective in miniature, with reproductions by the artist of his early paintings and renowned readymades which questioned the very definition of art itself. Like Dubuffet, Duchamp believed art should address the mind and not the eye; he rejected what he called "retinal art" — Impressionism, for example, or even Cubism — preferring to explore ideas rather than imitate appearances. This same attitude is a major strength and challenge of the Westons as collectors; despite their intention to approximate a historical survey of postwar art, they have exhibited a predilection for the cerebral and a distinct disregard for less intellectually difficult

movements such as Photorealism, or the visually ingratiating Pattern Painting that became popular in the late 1970s.

Both Duchamp and Cage were critical models for Johns, among many others, and their aloofness from subjectivity and sentiment reverberates in his choice of readymade subject matter in the famous target and flag paintings he produced in the late fifties. His lithograph in this exhibition, *#1* (1968), is typical of his deadpan iconographical themes, although there is still an attachment to a somewhat expressive handling of the medium. The numeral, a sign rather than a traditional still-life subject as such, is common, impersonal, two-dimensional, and utterly ordinary. Even the vestigial element of personal preference or choice in the singling out of a particular number, however, is undercut in Johns's etching *Numbers* (1967-69, no. 46), in which the entire set of numbers from zero to nine is presented. Moreover, the artist avoids any sense of differentiation or hierarchical value among the digits: superimposing the numbers ensures that no one of them occupies the first or privileged place.

Still more rigorous in their withdrawal of emotional or psychological overtones from the work of art are Minimalists such as Dorothea Rockburne, Robert Ryman, and Richard Tuttle. The formal purity and extreme understatement that characterizes their production has often been seen as a reaction to the heroic rhetoric of the New York School, with its implications of existential anxiety and its emphasis on the individual hand or touch of the artist. Yet Rockburne's minimal paper-fold pieces (no. 68), Ryman's white-on-white print, and Tuttle's spare wall-mounted sculptures (no. 88) are still handmade, unlike the industrially fabricated works by Carl Andre and Dan Flavin, which place the artist at one more remove from sensuous interaction with the medium. In floor pieces like *5, 7, Thick Aluminum Prime Couple* (1976, no. 4), Andre has reduced sculpture to its barest essentials, eliminating not only the pedestal but also the verticality that always tended to anthropomorphize even the most abstract sculptural form.

While Andre has selected wood blocks, firebricks, or metal plates as basic units of his spartan vocabulary, Flavin uses commercial light fixtures, fluorescent tubes displaced from their normal location on the ceiling to an artful position on the floor or wall. "His pieces," as critic Peter Schjeldahl has remarked, "are only art when installed and electrified; betweentimes they are just hardware."[18] *Untitled (Fondly to Helen)* (1976, no. 39) is ethereal and beautiful, with its own aura of radiance and color. Although it seems a contradiction in terms, Flavin is the romantic Minimalist, transforming a banal utility into sheer poetry; even the title has feeling. It is somewhat ironic, too, that minimalist artists, in their rejection of the chisel and the brush, their embrace of anonymity through readymade materials, have nevertheless achieved startling individuality. Andre's aluminum plates and Flavin's fluorescent fixtures have become signature substances, as telling of their authorship as any of De Kooning's spontaneous strokes.

Sol LeWitt's signature device is the grid; variations on it constitute nearly all his oeuvre, whether painted wood or aluminum in three dimensions, or chalk or graphite in two. Rational and geometric, his work has been called systemic and often depends on a premise which is first stated, then played out without the artist's intervention. "The artist's will," LeWitt has claimed, "is secondary to the process he initiates from the idea to completion. His willfulness may only be ego."[19] Like other Minimalists, LeWitt devalues not only subjectivity but also the actual crafting of the object, a procedure he generally leaves to others, privileging instead the concept of the work of art as it originates in the artist's mind. A conceptual artist par excellence, in the tradition of Duchamp and Cage, LeWitt declared early in his career that

"the idea becomes the Machine that makes the art."[20] His *Atlantic City Piece* (1971) consists of a set of instructions for a wall drawing anyone can make; its visual realization, which can vary in appearance according to the person following LeWitt's directions, exists in the Westons' home, in the Cincinnati Art Museum for the occasion of this exhibition, and could conceivably exist elsewhere as well. The work of art, however, resides in the idea rather than its rendering.

Minimalism and Pop were simultaneous movements, although Pop art, colorful and friendly, caught the public's attention sooner than the mute "primary structures" and "specific objects" of what was initially referred to as serial, literalist, or ABC art. While Minimalists and Pop artists alike jettisoned the values of Abstract Expressionism, they obviously did so in wildly different ways: Pop's warm affirmation of consumer culture and media celebrities in representational icons for our age is as unlike the cool, timeless abstractions of minimal art as anything could be. Reveling in the everyday, Robert Indiana, Claes Oldenburg, James Rosenquist, Tom Wesselmann, and Warhol went to the supermarket for their subjects, picked up the comics, drove down the highway, or took in a movie. Their embrace of commercial art, brand names, and advertising, which had precedents in Johns and Rauschenberg and in Dada artists such as Duchamp and Kurt Schwitters, flew in the face of "high art" and good taste. "I am for an art," Oldenburg proclaimed boldly in the early sixties, "that does something other than sit on its ass in a museum....I am for art that is smoked, like a cigarette, smells, like a pair of shoes....that is put on and taken off, like pants, which develops holes, like socks, which is eaten, like a piece of pie...."[21]

There is an adolescent defiance in these words, and it seems hard to believe that Pop has come of age, that a quarter of a century has passed since the Westons first found Oldenburg's beguiling *Box of Shirts* (1962, no. 59) difficult to like. And perhaps since his death in 1987, Warhol has come to be understood more fully for the meaning of his cultural production, beyond what appeared to be the sheer mischief of elevating, in works like the Westons' *Soup Can* (1962, no. 95), Campbell's cream of mushroom to the status of subject matter for easel painting. Beneath his adulation of television, movie stars, and fashion was the realization that photography had changed our experience of the world, that what we know in this electronic age comes to us not first hand but mediated – taped or filmed, broadcast, transmitted, printed, reproduced ad infinitum. Warhol's sources are thus invariably photographs, not objects or models, and his silkscreened *Elizabeth Taylor* (1965) reproduces an image from a magazine, which is itself a reproduction from a publicity shot of an actress whose personal identity is obscured behind a mask of makeup and glamor.

Warhol, too, wore a mask, which concealed the real Andrew Warhola, Jr. but mirrored our society. His prediction that in the future everyone would be famous for fifteen minutes, his professed desire to be a machine, and his celebration of the boring and the ordinary were Warhol's ways of leveling an outmoded hierarchy of artistic values exalting notions of individuality and genius.[22] His are some of the most relevant cultural insights offered in this exhibition of the Weston collection, in which art is less a traditional mirror of nature and the world than an index of human attitudes about that world. In assembling this collection, over a period of years, Alice and Harris Weston have demonstrated what another collector of modern art has claimed: "We need art's organizing power . . . to clarify our perceptions and conceptions about existence, life, and death."[23] And in parting for a time with their cherished works of art, in which Harris Weston especially takes such pride, in order to share them on this occasion with a museum audience, these inspired collectors have also indicated their belief that "aesthetic pleasure is always multiplied by division."[24]

— Sue Taylor

Notes

1. Katharine Kuh, "An Appreciation" in *The Mr. & Mrs. Joseph Randall Shapiro Collection* (Chicago: Art Institute of Chicago, 1985), 15.

2. See Wassily Kandinsky, *Concerning the Spiritual in Art*, trans. M. T. H. Sadler (New York: Dover Publications, 1977), chapter III.

3. See Rose-Carol Washton Long, "Kandinsky and Abstraction: The Role of the Hidden Image," *Artforum* 10 (June 1972): 42-49.

4. Kandinsky, *Concerning the Spiritual*, chapter IV.

5. Wassily Kandinsky and Franz Marc, eds., *The Blaue Reiter Almanac* [English translation] (New York: Viking Press, 1974).

6. "Rafael Ferrer: An Interview" [conducted by Michael Flanagan and Joshua Kind] in *Rafael Ferrer* (DeKalb, Ill.: Swen Parson Gallery, Northern Illinois University, 1982), unpaginated.

7. For two excellent accounts of the Surrealists' embrace of non-Western art, see James Clifford, "On Ethnographic Surrealism," *Comparative Studies in Society and History* 23 (1981): 539-564, and Evan Maurer, "Dada and Surrealism" in William Rubin, ed., *"Primitivism" in 20th Century Art*, vol. 2 (New York: Museum of Modern Art, 1984), 534-613. For Dubuffet's "Anti-Cultural Positions" lecture delivered at the Arts Club of Chicago on December 20, 1951, see the exhibition catalogue *Dubuffet and the Anticulture* (New York: Richard L. Feigen & Co., 1969) or the transcription published by Barbara Rose in *Arts Magazine* 53 (April 1979): 156-157.

8. Jean Dubuffet quoted in Reinhold Heller, "'A Swan Only Sings at the Moment It Disappears': Jean Dubuffet and Art at the Edge of Non-Art" in *Jean Dubuffet: Forty Years of His Art* (Chicago: David and Alfred Smart Gallery, University of Chicago, 1984), 23.

9. Artist's statement in the exhibition brochure *Alice Weston* (Cincinnati: University of Cincinnati Health Sciences Library, n.d.).

10. Robert Hobbs quoted in Lucy Lippard, *Overlay: Contemporary Art and the Art of Prehistory* (New York: Pantheon Books, 1983), 225.

11. Lippard, *Overlay,* 138.

12. Budd Hopkins, "The Drawings of Willem de Kooning," *Drawing* 5 (March/April 1984): 124.

13. William Seitz, *Hans Hofmann* (New York: Museum of Modern Art, 1963), 56.

14. Nicholas Fox Weber, "Josef Albers" in John R. Lane and Susan C. Larsen, eds., *Abstract Painting and Sculpture in America 1927-1944* (Pittsburgh: Museum of Art, Carnegie Institute, 1983), 47.

15. Robert Rauschenberg quoted in National Collection of Fine Arts, *Robert Rauschenberg* (Washington, D. C.: National Collection of Fine Arts, Smithsonian Institution, 1976), 27

16. Calvin Tomkins, *Off the Wall: Robert Rauschenberg*

and the Art World of Our Time (New York: Penguin Books, 1980), 103.

17. John Cage quoted in Anthony Tommasini, "The Zest of the Uninteresting," *New York Times*, 23 April 1989, H27.

18. Peter Schjeldahl, "Minimalism" in *1985 Carnegie International* (Pittsburgh: Museum of Art, Carnegie Institute, 1985), 68.

19. Sol LeWitt, "Sentences on Conceptual Art," *Art-Language* 1 (May 1969): 11.

20. LeWitt, "Paragraphs on Conceptual Art," *Artforum* 5 (June 1967): 80.

21. Claes Oldenburg, "I am for an art... ," from *Store Days, Documents from the Store (1961) and Ray Gun Theater (1962)*, selected by Oldenburg and Emmett Williams, New York, 1967. Reprinted in Ellen H. Johnson, ed., *American Artists on Art 1940 to 1980* (New York: Harper & Row, 1982), 98.

22. Sue Taylor, "Andy Warhol: An Artist as Elusive as His Art," *Chicago Sun-Times*, 12 April 1987, "Show Section," 2.

23. Joseph Randall Shapiro, "Introduction" in *The Shapiro Collection*, 9.

24. Ibid.

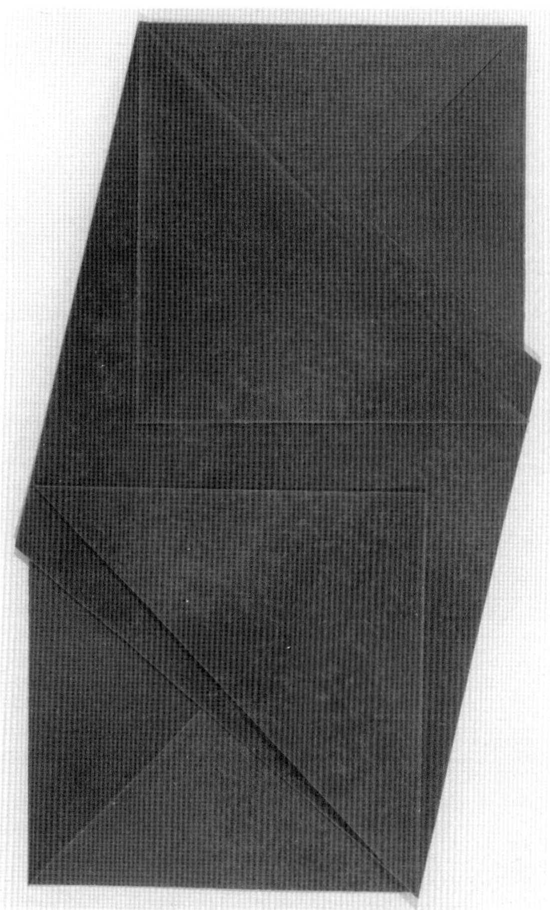

68. Dorothea Rockburne, Copal #6, n.d.

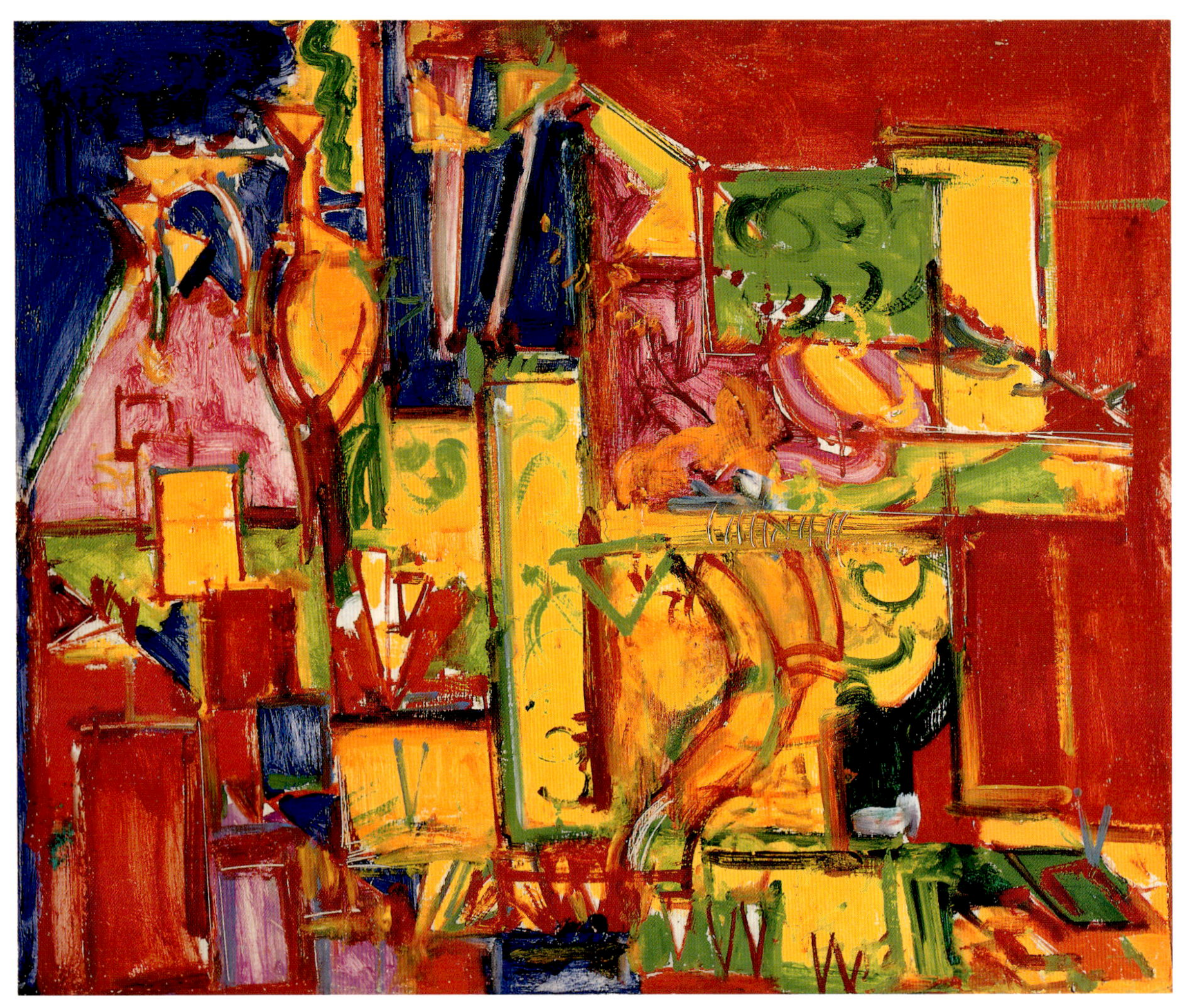

42. Hans Hofmann, Untitled, 1942

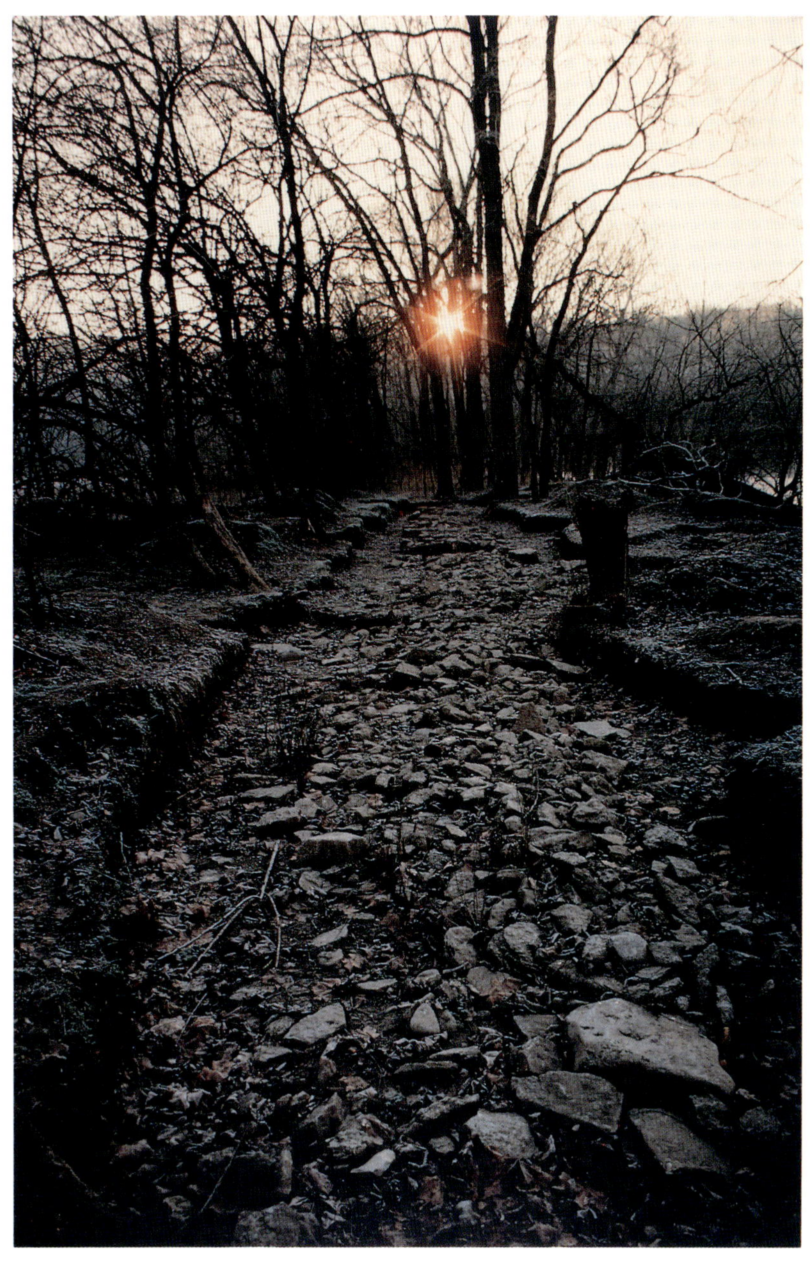

103. Alice Weston, Winter Solstice, 1985

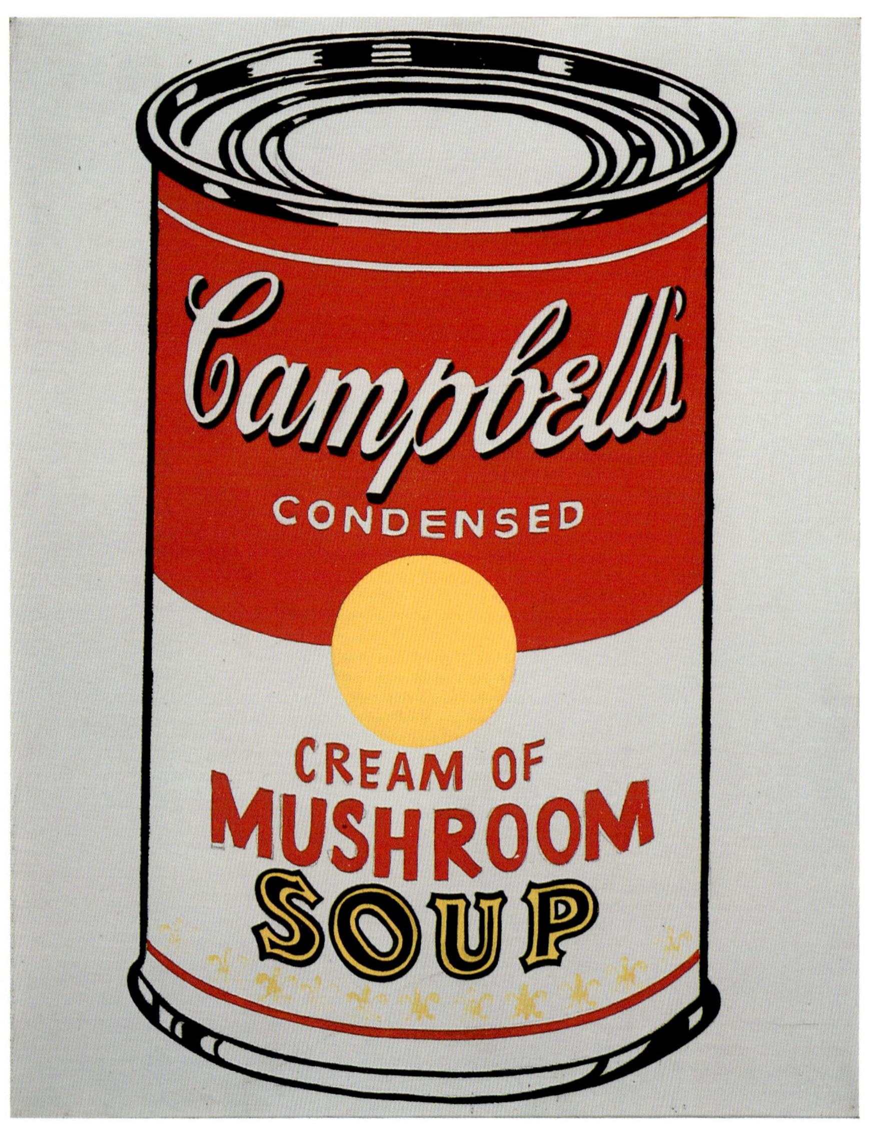

95. Andy Warhol, Soup Can, 1962

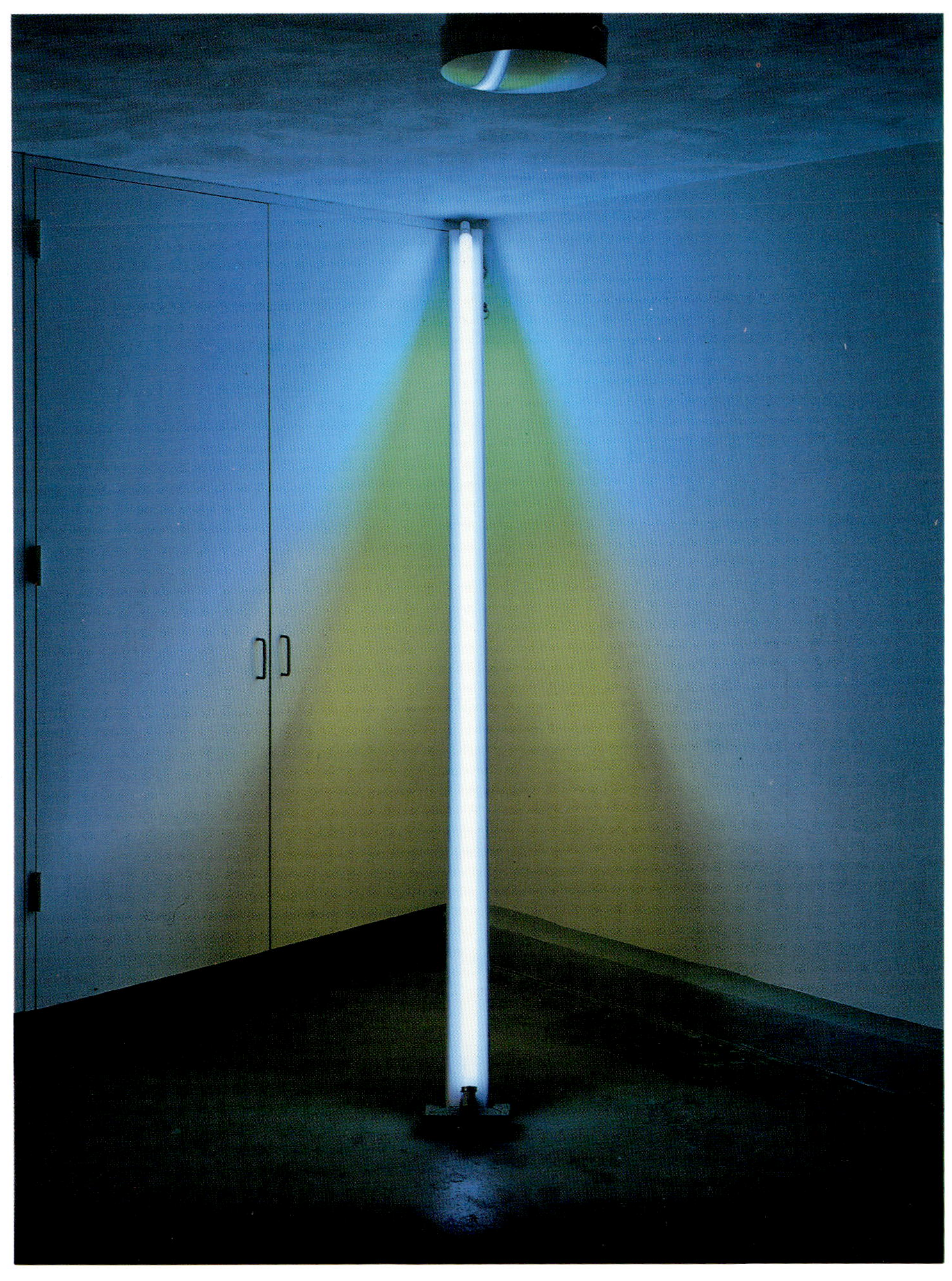

39. Dan Flavin, Untitled (Fondly to Helen), 1976

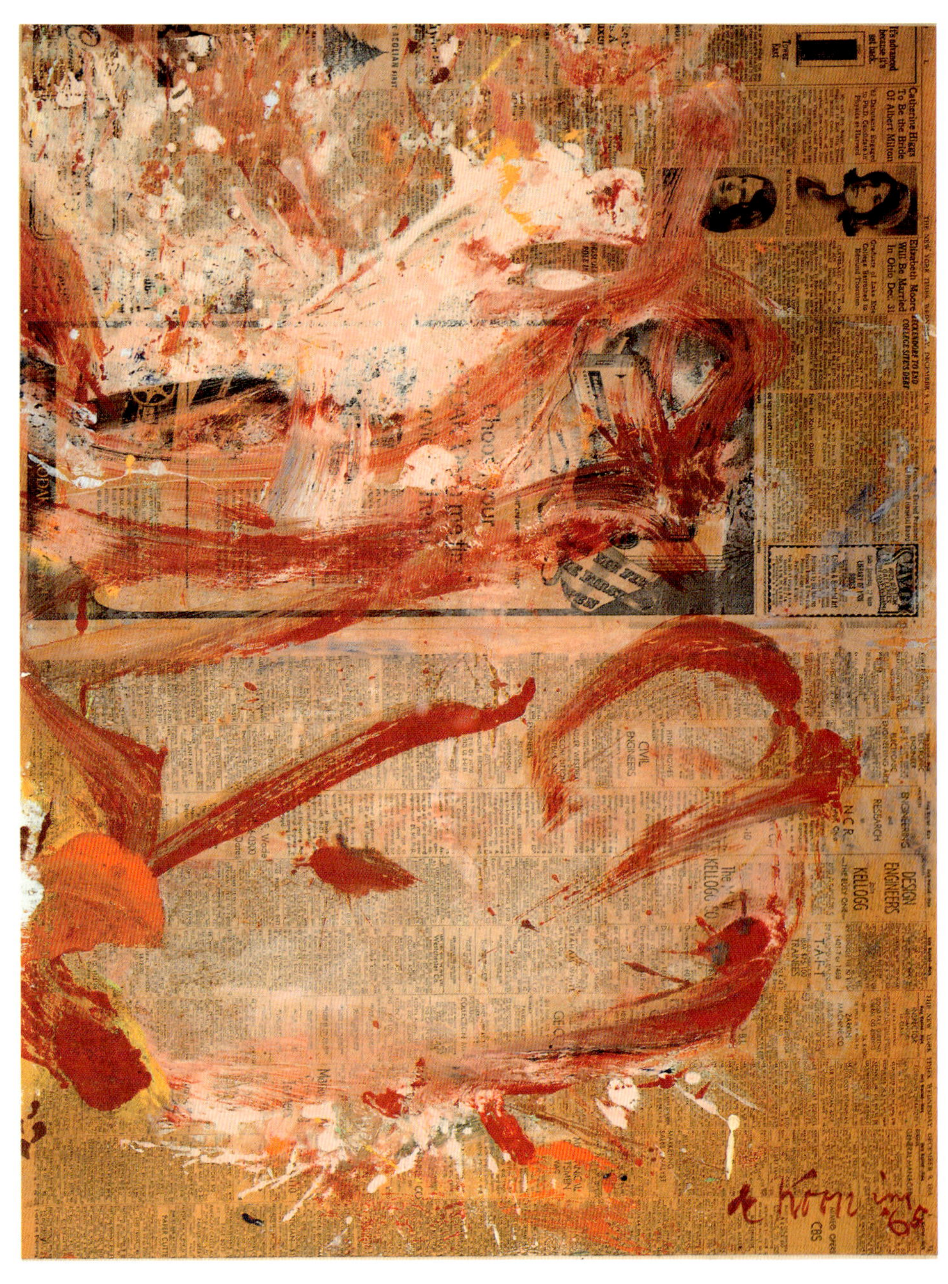

21. Willem de Kooning, Torso or Cross-Legged Woman, 1965

Checklist

1 **Josef Albers**
Deep Tune, 1964
Oil on masonite, 48 x 48 in.

2 **Josef Albers**
Study for Homage to the Square Blue
Spring, 1959
Oil on masonite, 18 x 18 in.

3 **Josef Albers**
White Setting, 1959
Oil on masonite, 24 x 24 in.

4 **Carl Andre**
5,7, Thick Aluminum Prime Couple, 1976
Aluminum, $11\frac{7}{8}$ x $11\frac{7}{8}$ in. each

5 **Louise Behr**
Pink Lady, 1964
Watercolor, 15 x 11 in.

6 **Harry Bertoia**
Diagonal Sound Piece, 1961
Bronze, 18 x 10 x 6 in.

7 **Harry Bertoia**
Golden Towers, 1963
Gilded rods on bronze base, 9 x $4\frac{1}{2}$ x $1\frac{1}{2}$ in.

8 **Harry Bertoia**
Sound Piece, 1961
Bronze, 47 x $11\frac{1}{2}$ x $11\frac{1}{2}$ in.

9 **Harry Bertoia**
Untitled, 1966
Aluminum spray rods, 37 x 10 x 10 in.

10 **Max Bill**
Untitled, 1961-63
Gold plate over lead, 13 x 13 x 13 in.

11 **Jack Boulton**
Tortola, 1986
Watercolor, 22 x 14 in.

12 **John Cage**
Adjourned Game, 1973
Pencil on paper, $8\frac{1}{2}$ x 11 in.

13 **John Cage**
Not Wanting to Say Anything About
Marcel . . . , 1969
Plexigrams I-VIII, 14 x 20 x $\frac{1}{8}$ in. each

14 **John Cage**
Not Wanting to Say Anything About
Marcel . . . ,1969
Lithograph A & B
27½ x 40 in.

15 **John Cage**
Thirty Drawings by Thoreau, 1974
Merce Cunningham Portfolio
Color silkscreen on Japanese paper,
20 x 30 in.

16 **John Chamberlain**
Untitled, 1968
Galvanized steel, 20½ x 28 x 15½ in.

17 **Christo**
Wrapped Documents, 1983
Plastic wrapped paper tied with cord,
14 x 8½ x 1 in.

18 **Jean Corbero**
Two Squares, 1968
Bronze, 14 x 14 x 4 in.

19 **Joseph Cornell**
The Sun Series, 1957
Box with objects, 6¼ x 10½ x 4 in.

20 **Willem de Kooning**
Rome Series, 1959
Oil on rag paper, 27½ x 39 in.

21 **Willem de Kooning**
Torso or Cross-Legged Woman, 1965
Oil on paper, mounted, 28½ x 22 in.

22 **Jim Dine**
Marlboro Collage, 1965
Lithograph, 23½ x 19½ in.

23 **Jim Dine**
The Studio: Red Devil Color Chart #1, 1963
Oil on canvas, 84 x 60 in.

24 **Jim Dine**
Shower #4, 1962
Collage, pastel and wash, 37 x 22½ in.

25 **Jean Dubuffet**
Exodus, 1961
Ink and wash drawing, 10 x 13 in.

26 **Jean Dubuffet**
Jardin de Terre, 1959
Lithograph, 25¼ x 18 in.

27 **Jean Dubuffet**
Mycelium, 1959
Lithograph, 25¼ x 18 in.

28 **Jean Dubuffet**
Paysage Exuberant, 1954
Collage, 19 x 23 in.

29 **Jean Dubuffet**
Poudroiement, 1959
Lithograph, 25¼ x 18 in.

30 **Marcel Duchamp**
Czech Check, 1965
Card, 5 x 2½ in.

31 **Marcel Duchamp**
The Clock in Profile, 1964
Lithograph and collage, 11 x 8½ in.

32 **Marcel Duchamp**
The Coffee Grinder, 1947
Etching after oil painting of 1911, 7 x 5 in.

33 **Marcel Duchamp**
Roto-Relief, 1965
Cardboard disks on velvet box machine,
15 x 14½ x 4½ in.

34 **Marcel Duchamp**
Valise, 1955-68
Paris-Milan edition, Box with objects,
16 x 15 x 4 in. (closed), 16 x 46 x 38 in.
(open)

35 **Rafael Ferrer**
Boat, 1972
Wood and neon, 12 x 5 x 3 ft.

36 **Rafael Ferrer**
Es un Profeta, 1975
Metal, wire, crayons, wood, beads, acrylic,
48 x 23 x 19 in.

37 **Rafael Ferrer**
Face, 1973
Crayon on brown paper, 12 x 9½ in.

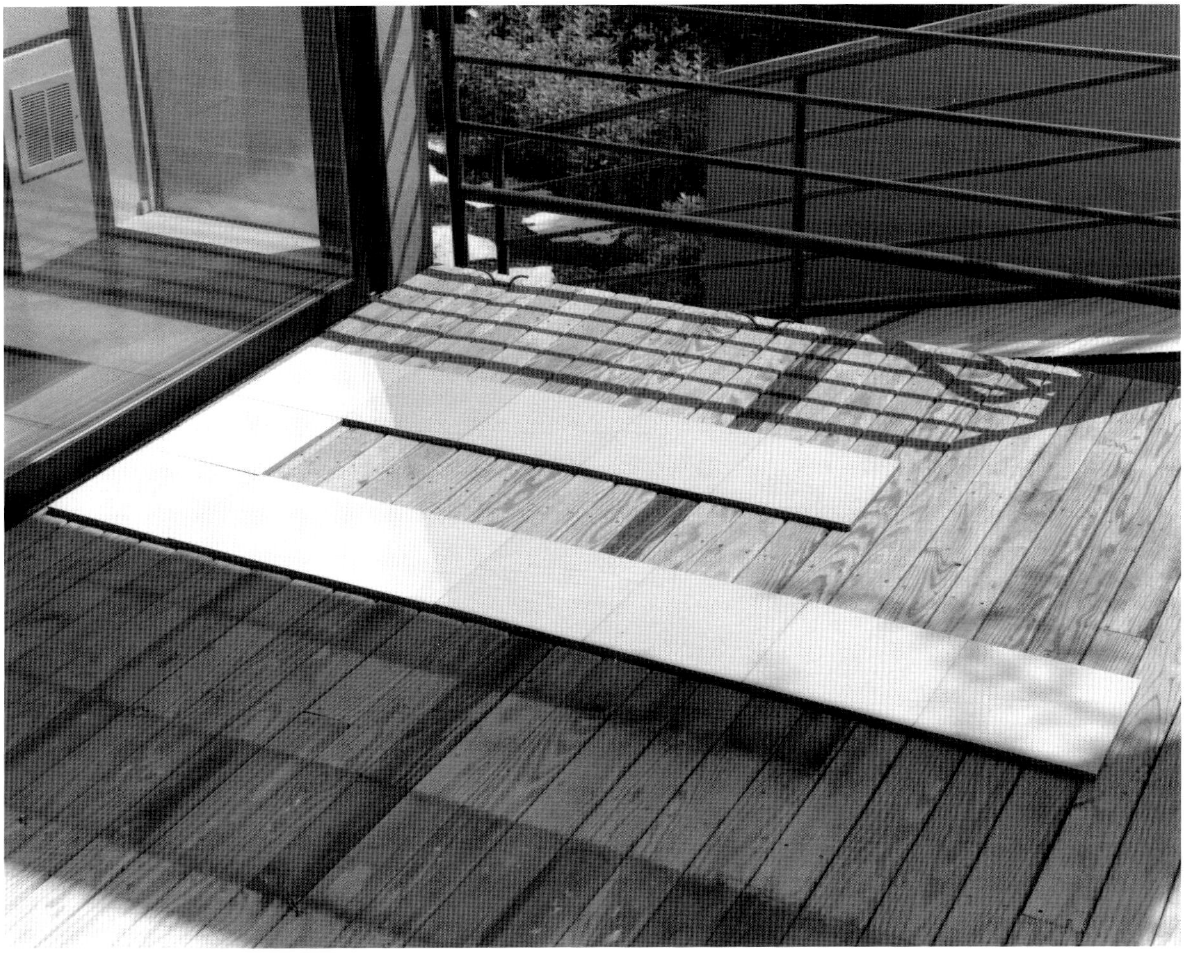

4. Carl Andre, 5, 7, Thick Aluminum Prime Couple, 1976

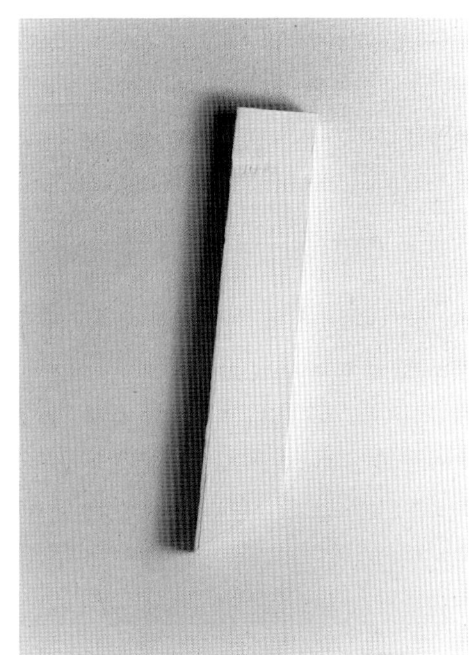

88. Richard Tuttle, Cincinnati Pieces, 1975

24. Jim Dine, Shower #4, 1962

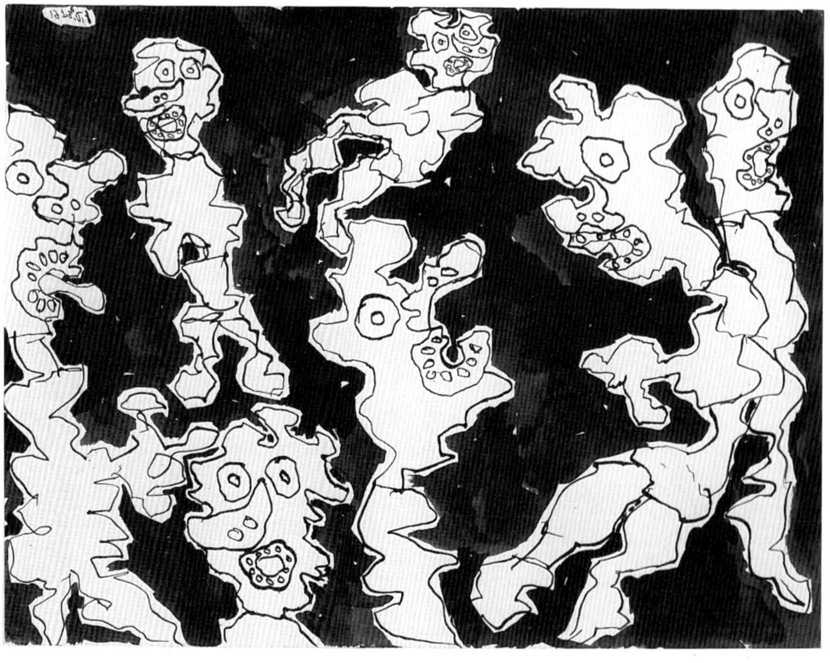

29. Jean Dubuffet, Poudroiement, 1959

38 **Rafael Ferrer**
Installation Drawing for Boat, 1974
Crayon on paper, 11 x 8½ in.

39 **Dan Flavin**
Untitled (Fondly to Helen), 1976
Blue, green, and yellow fluorescent light,
8 ft., 2 ft., and 4 ft.

40 **Etienne Hajdu**
Untitled, 1958
Engraving, 25 x 19½ in.

41 **Richard Hamilton**
Five Tyres Remoulded, 1972
Relief in white synthetic rubber with
screen prints on mylar, 24 x 33½ in.

42 **Hans Hofmann**
Untitled, 1942
Oil on board, 24 x 30 in.

43 **Robert Indiana**
Fork, 1962
Oil on canvas, 12 x 12 in.

44 **Jasper Johns**
#1, 1968
Lithograph, 37 x 30 in.

45 **Jasper Johns**
M.D., 1974
Merce Cunningham Portfolio
Die-cut stencil on die-cut stencil paper,
22 x 18 in.

46 **Jasper Johns**
Numbers, 1967-69
Etching and open hit from first etchings,
portfolio printed on French watermarked
paper, 26 x 19½ in.

47 **Wassily Kandinsky**
Simple, 1916
Watercolor, 4½ x 6 in.

48 **Franz Kline**
Untitled, 1957-58
Oil and ink on cardboard, 9¼ x 13½ in.

49 **Sol LeWitt**
Atlantic City Piece, 1971
Ink drawing, 5 x 5 in.

50 **Robert Mallary**
Quad IV, 1970
Laminated slabs of computer-determined
marble, 11 x 12 x 6 in., (6 x 8 x 6 in. base)

51 **Joan Miró**
Untitled (I-91 of Series II/XII), n.d.
Hand-colored drawing on lithograph,
5½ x 4½ in.

52 **Joan Miró**
Untitled (II-70 of Series II/XII), n.d.
Hand-colored drawing on lithograph,
5½ x 4½ in.

53 **Joan Miró**
Untitled (VI-74 of Series II/XII), n.d.
Hand-colored drawing on lithograph,
5½ x 4½ in.

54 **Joan Miró**
Untitled (VIII-76 of Series II/XII), n.d.
Hand-colored drawing on lithograph,
5½ x 4½ in.

55 **Joan Miró**
Untitled (XI-79 of Series II/XII), n.d.
Hand-colored drawing on lithograph,
5½ x 4½ in.

56 **Henry Moore**
Untitled (Prometheus Series), n.d.
Lithograph, 13½ x 9½ in.

57 **Robert Morris**
Untitled, 1974
Merce Cunningham Portfolio
One-color silkscreen on Dutch etching
paper, 22 x 30 in.

58 **Bruce Nauman**
Caned Dance, 1974
Merce Cunningham Portfolio
Three-color lithograph, 22 x 30 in.

59 **Claes Oldenburg**
Box of Shirts, 1962
Oil on canvas, stuffed; boxed in wood
10 x 13 x 20 in.

60 **Claes Oldenburg**
Sailboat Thinking of Q, 1976
Lithograph, 16 x 12 in.

61 **Francis Picabia**
Lampe Cristal, 1922
Watercolor and ink, 24 x 29 in.

62 **Robert Rauschenberg**
Cunningham Relief, 1974
Merce Cunningham Portfolio
Embossing with hand-rubbed half-tone
on paper, 30 x 22½ in.

63 **Robert Rauschenberg**
Shades, 1964
Lithograph object, Plexiglas on frame,
15 x 14 x 11½ in.

64 **Man Ray**
N for Nothing, 1958
Metal chain on board, 13 x 8½ in.

65 **Man Ray**
Untitled, 1958
Oil on board, 9½ x 7½ in.

66 **George Rickey**
Single Rectangle, 1968
Brushed stainless steel, 16 x 8 x 15 in.

67 **George Rickey**
Three Lines Contrapuntal II, 1967
Kinetic sculpture in stainless steel,
36 x 1 x 3½ in.

68 **Dorothea Rockburne**
Copal #6, n.d.
Draft paper, varnish, blue pencil,
30¼ x 40¼ in.

69 **Dorothea Rockburne**
Paper Fold, Etchings, 1972
Paper, 30 x 38 in.

70 **Dorothea Rockburne**
Paper Fold Piece R.P. #4, 1973
Black crayon on white rice paper,
30 x 40 in.

71 **James Rosenquist**
Light Bulb, 1966
Lithograph, 22½ x 22½ in.

72 **Georges Rouault**
Ideal, n.d.
Lithograph, 12 x 9 in.

73 **Robert Ryman**
Untitled, 1971
Lithograph, 21⅞ x 21⅞ in.

74 **Kurt Schwitters**
Red Labels, n.d.
Collage, 8 x 6 in.

75 **George Segal**
Untitled, 1965
Pastel, 18 x 12 in.

76 **Robert Smithson**
Circle, 1973
Fossilized shale, 18 x 11 in.

77 **Robert Smithson**
Spiral Jetty, Great Salt Lake, 1970
Pencil, 12 x 9 in.

78 **Alan Sonfist**
Heat Interference Pattern, n.d.
Copper, 12 x 12 in.

79 **Alan Sonfist**
Heat Interference Pattern, n.d.
On zinc, 12 x 12 in.

80 **Alan Sonfist**
Micro-Organisms, n.d.
Micro-organisms on canvas, 63 x 15 in.

81 **Alan Sonfist**
Twig, n.d.
Twig, leaf, 4 x 6 in.

82 **Alan Sonfist**
Walking Stone, 1978.
Stone pebble on ceramic track,
17¾ x 3 x ¾ in.

83 **Pierre Soulages**
Untitled, n.d.
Color lithograph, 25½ x 19½ in.

84 **Julian Stanczak**
Dedicated to the Cincinnati Print and
Drawing Circle, 1971
Serigraph on Fabriano paper,
25¼ x 30⅞ in.

81. Alan Sonfist, Twig, n.d.

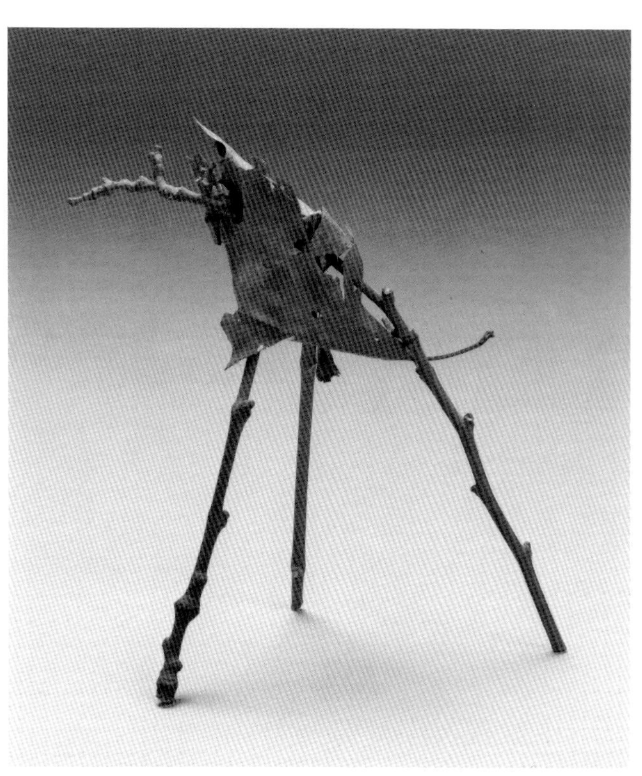

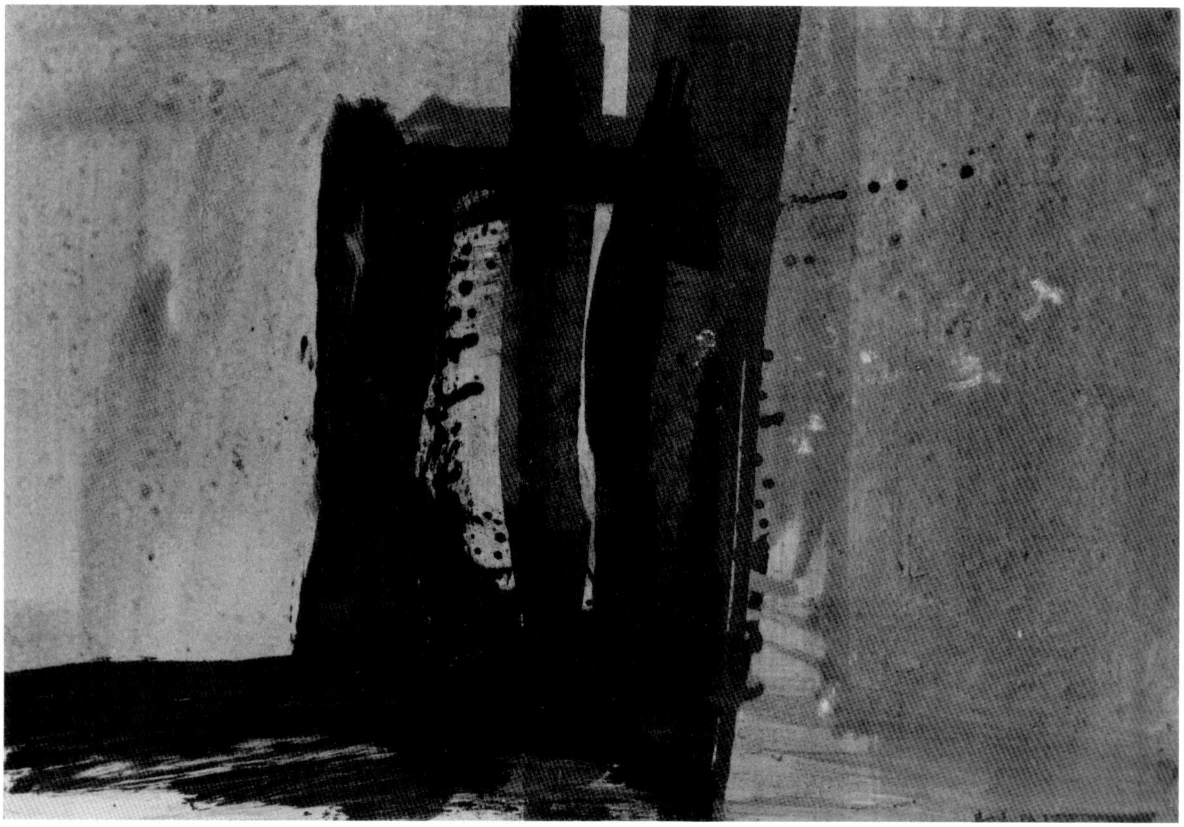

48. Franz Kline, Untitled, 1957-58

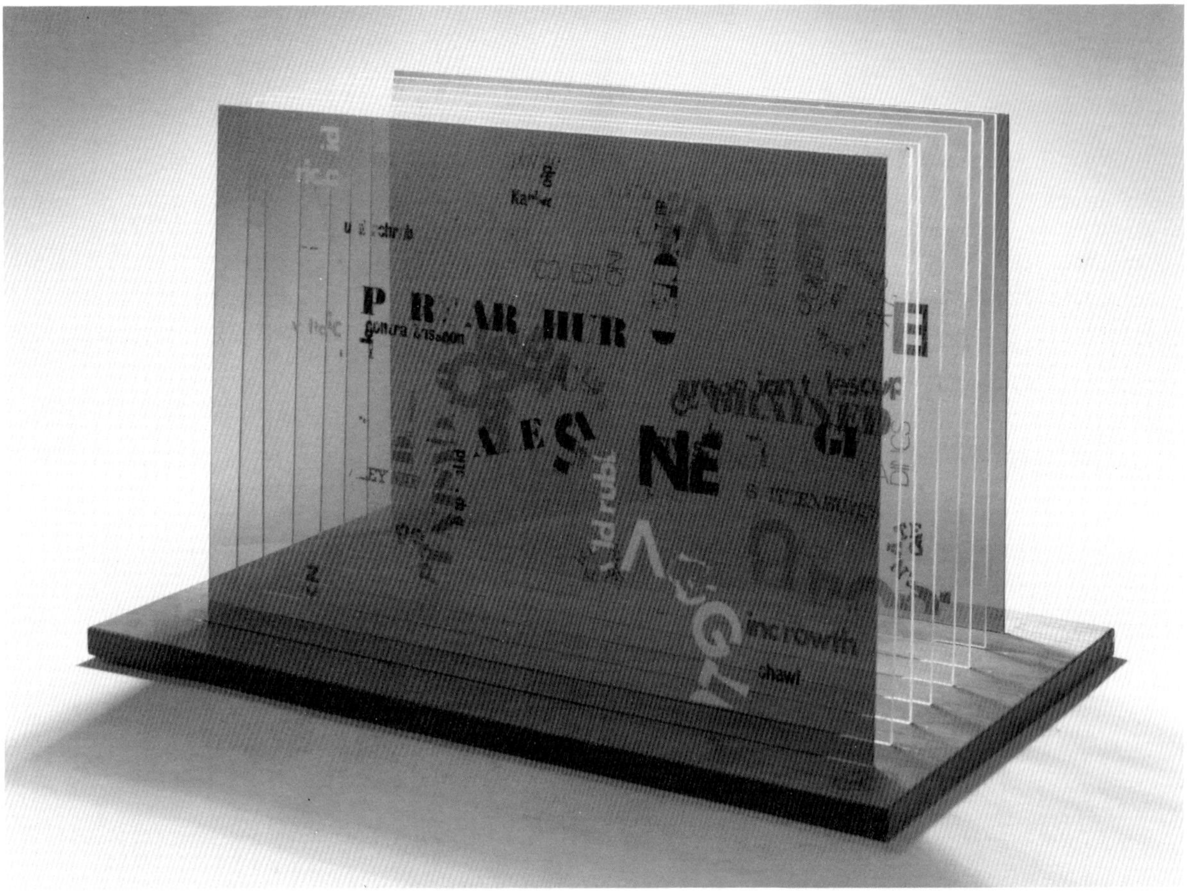

13. John Cage, Not Wanting to Say Anything
about Marcel . . . , 1969

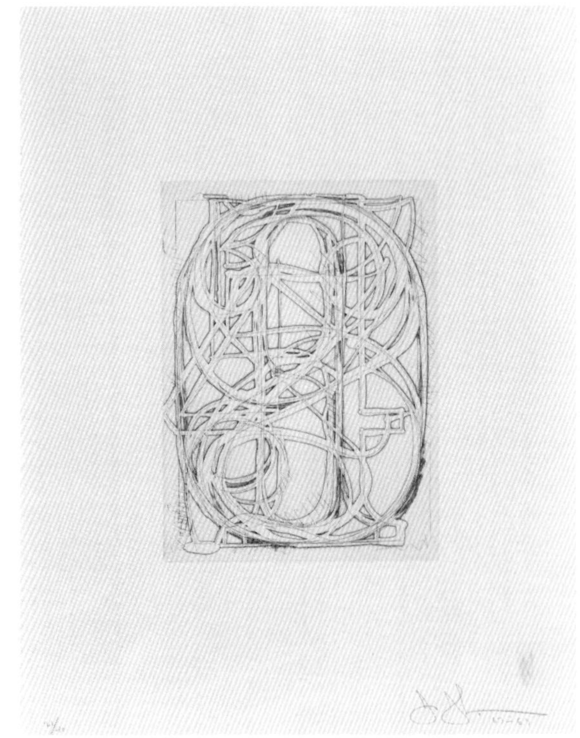

46. Jasper Johns, Numbers, 1967-69

85 **Saul Steinberg**
Riverhead Stipulation, 1966
Ink drawing, 24 x 30 in.

86 **Frank Stella**
Furg, 1975
Merce Cunningham Portfolio
Lithograph and color silkscreen on paper,
17 x 22 in.

87 **Michael Tracy**
Texas Gulf Drawing, 1973
Paper and plastic, 48 x 35 in.

88 **Richard Tuttle**
Cincinnati Pieces, 1975
10 painted wood pieces, 14½ -
24 x 3½ x 1½ in.

89 **Richard Tuttle**
Wire Piece, 1978
Wire and pencil, 12 x 6 x 5 in.

90 **Victor Vasarely**
Untitled, 1968.
Screen print, 26 x 20 in.

91 **Jacques Villon**
Untitled, 1946
Etching, 3 x 5 in.

92 **Andy Warhol**
Elizabeth Taylor, 1965
Silkscreen on paper, 24 x 24 in.

93 **Andy Warhol**
Flowers, 1964
Silkscreen on paper, 24 x 24½ in.

94 **Andy Warhol**
Merce, 1974
Merce Cunningham Portfolio
One-color silkscreen on floral paper, 30 x 20 in.

95 **Andy Warhol**
Soup Can, 1962
Oil on canvas, 20 x 16 in.

96 **Tom Wesselmann**
Great American Still Life #6, 1962
Collage on board, 24 x 31 in.

97 **Alice Weston**
Cellular Landscape, 1971
Mixed media, 72 x 24 x 24 in.

98 **Alice Weston**
The First Gleam of Summer, 1985
Photograph, 30 x 40 in.

99 **Alice Weston**
Inner Journey, 1987
Video and performance

100 **Alice Weston**
Inside Tracks, 1988
Mixed media, 14 x 14 x 14 in.

101 **Alice Weston**
Stringy Quartet #3, 1971-74
Crystal microphotograph, liquid
crystal light box,
16 x 20 in.

102 **Alice Weston**
Ultra-marine and Black, 1971
Monoprints, 26 x 40 in. each

103 **Alice Weston**
Winter Solstice, 1985
Photograph, 30 x 40 in.

104 **Lin Show Yu**
Untitled, 1961
Oil on canvas and aluminum, 50 x 30 in.

105 **Christopher Makos**
Portrait of Alice Weston, 1989
Photograph, 8 x 10 in.

106 **Mark di Suvero**
Tock, 1971
Steel, 51 x 47 x 36 in.

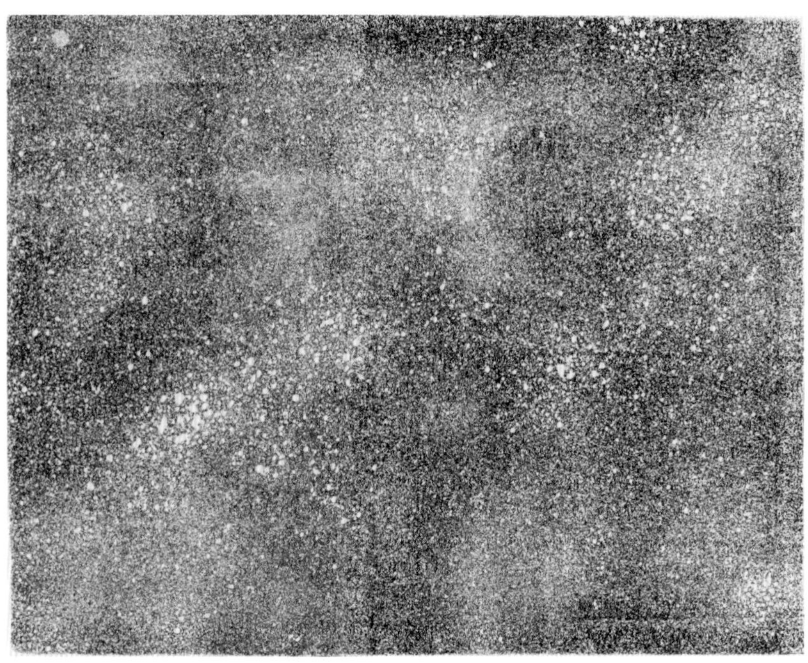

25. Jean Dubuffet, Exodus, 1961

33. Marcel Duchamp, Roto-Relief, 1965

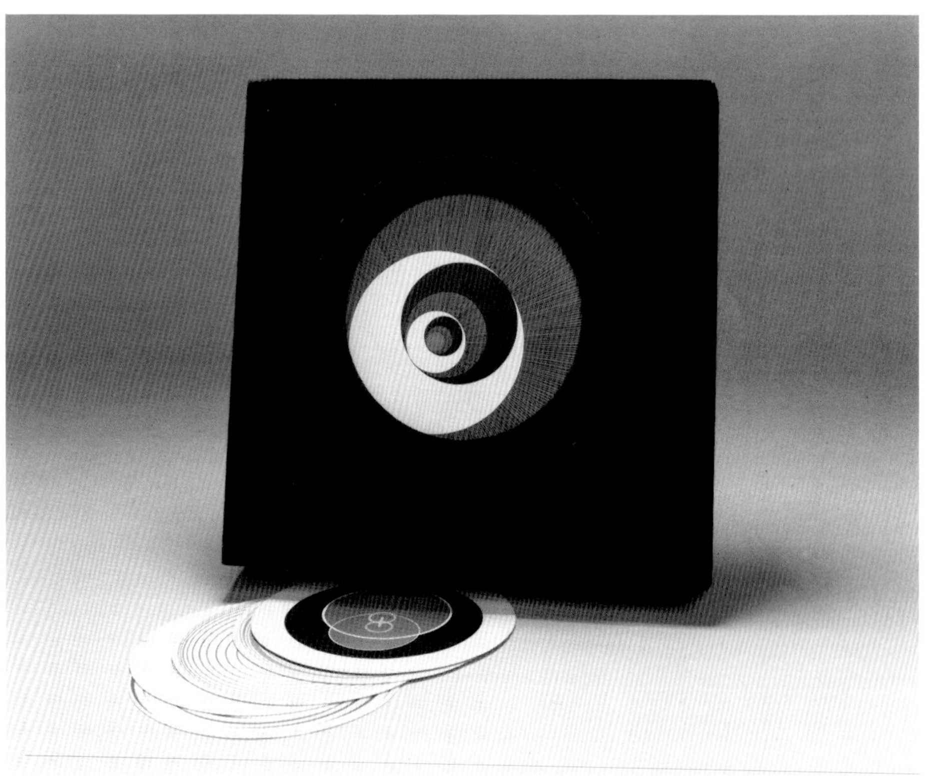

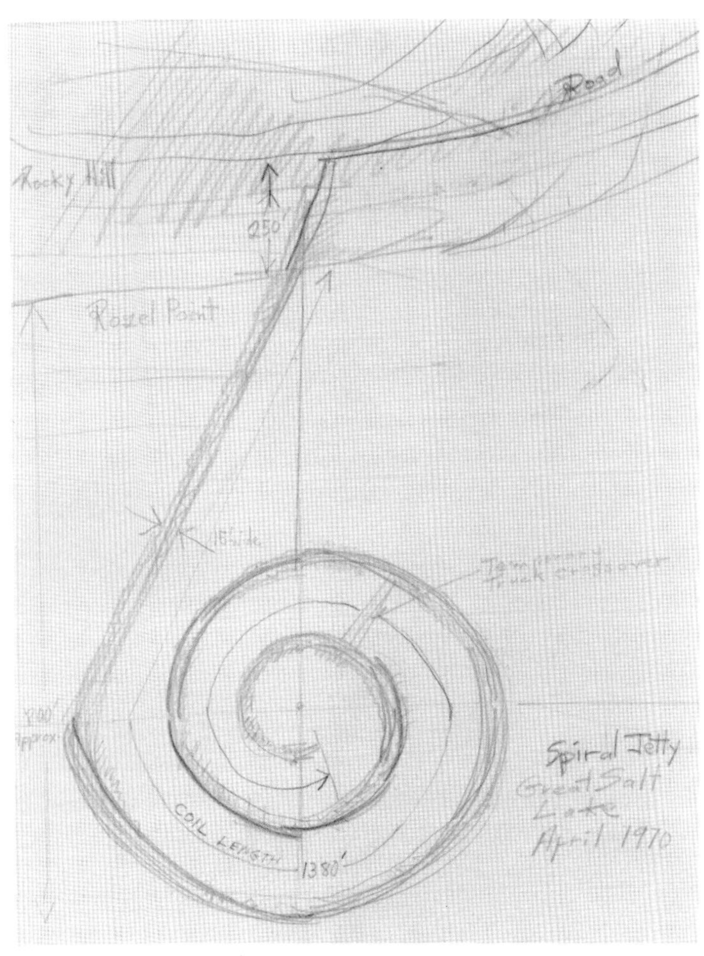

77. Robert Smithson, Spiral Jetty, Great Salt Lake, 1970

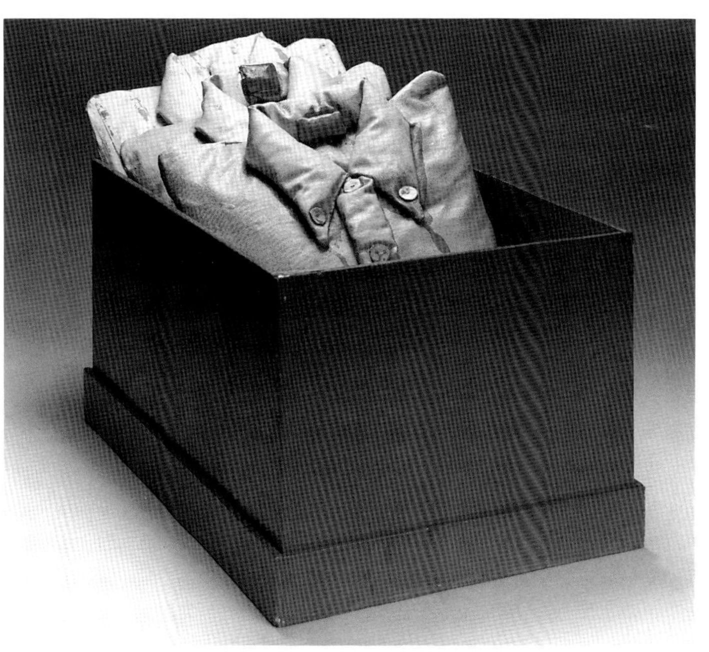

59. Claes Oldenburg, Box of Shirts, 1962

17. Christo, Wrapped Documents, 1983, Copyright Christo 1983

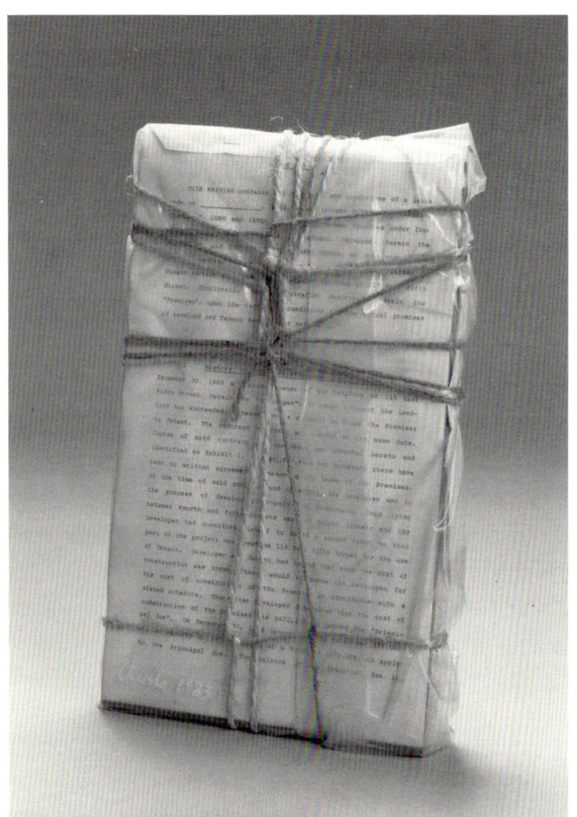

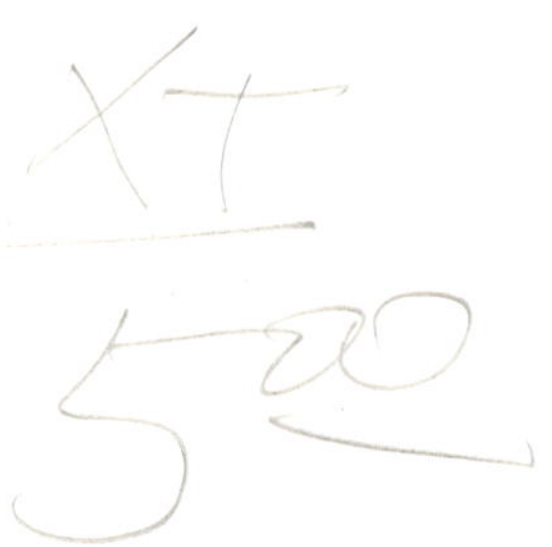

63. Robert Rauschenberg, Shades, 1964

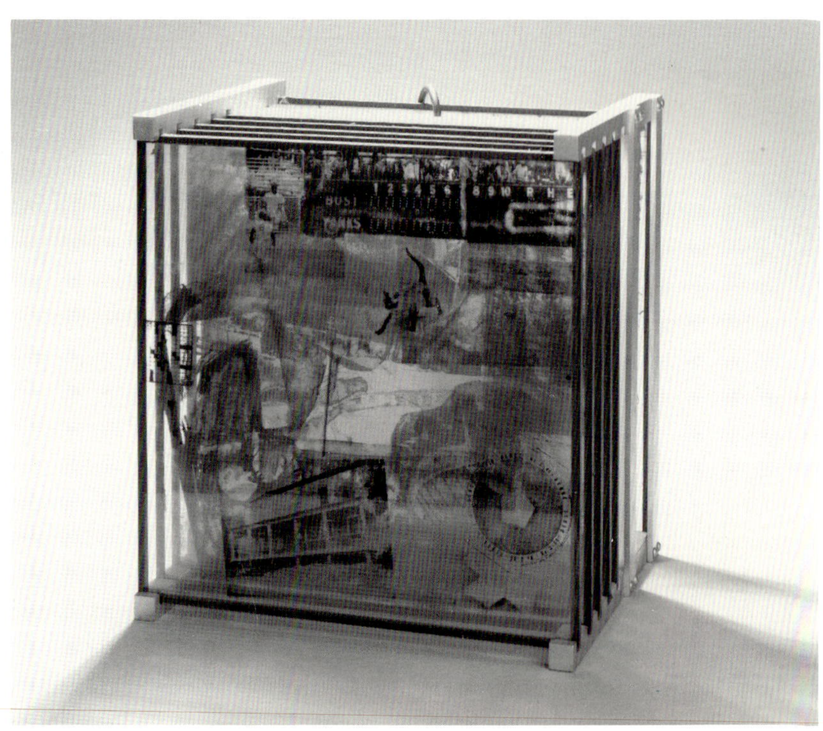